BIG BLUE SKY

A Celebration of Norfolk

Barrie Lawrence

ISBN 978-1-915292-20-9

Printed in Great Britain by
Biddles Books Limited, King's Lynn, Norfolk

To Wendy,
My wife, lover, best friend, partner in life,
and adopted daughter of Norfolk.

Preface

"I blame the Women's Institute!"

That has been my usual answer to the question, "How did you come to write books?" I was a young dentist, and a patient asked me if I would speak at a meeting of her Women's Institute. I felt it could be a novel experience, and a break from the routine, albeit enjoyable, of life in the surgery. I duly attended, hummed and la-la'd my way through *Jerusalem*, applauded the lady who had just celebrated her 93rd birthday, and then bored them to tears with detailed accounts of the structure of dentine and enamel, the chemical composition of amalgam, etc. until – I mentioned that the most common way for people to lose their false teeth is by vomiting them down the toilet and flushing too soon afterwards. Suddenly everybody woke up and the meeting became alive. I received other invitations to speak at similar meetings, and left out everything technical, and spoke solely on false teeth down the toilet, false teeth chewed by a dog, false teeth shared by a couple, and similar stories. My speaking engagements took off, and I found myself at ladies luncheon clubs, dinner meetings of all descriptions, and eventually at quite formal dinners of one of our two main political parties. And I was quite often asked, "When will you write a book?" So, I blame the Women's Institute.

In addition to being a dentist to several patients who lost their false teeth down the toilet, I am a practising Christian. In fact, the latter is first and foremost in my life, and my first book concerned my faith. But after that, I wrote a book covering the stories I relate when entertaining people at dinners. Other books followed, and until recently, there were six – three concerning my faith, and three light anecdotal concerning my life as a dentist. Also, one of them, *A Dentist's Story*, has been translated into Farsi, and is on sale in Iran under the title, *Holy Teeth!* And that, I thought, was the end of my career as an author.

Life is busy, even well into my retirement years. We have six daughters and twenty grandchildren living in five different countries, and so we travel. Additionally, I am very involved in a fellowship called the *Full Gospel Businessmen* (FGB) both locally, regionally and nationally, and so that too involves time and travel. How did I ever find time to work? And then the pandemic struck. I must confess that Wendy and I loved the change in routine. We had been advised to have a three-month sabbatical from church and FGB, but felt we were unable. And then, as it were, heaven opened, and we received a twelve-month sabbatical. Here in Norfolk, the sun shone out of a great big cobalt blue sky, and we walked and walked. We discovered new footpaths that meandered along the banks of our local river Bure. We crossed fields and streams, following tracks and bridleways, and discovered curiously named lanes such as Granny Bard's Lane, Muck Lane, Nowhere Lane, and dozens more. And as we walked, I reflected on my seventy-plus year love affair with the county of my birth – Norfolk. I chuckled as I remembered friends from my childhood, of schooldays from a dim and distant past, and yet full of fun. And I started scribbling, without ever intending to write yet another book. But that is what happened, and now, as the restrictions of what has been a truly dreadful time for so many (we have lost both friends and family during the last twelve months) are eased, it is my pleasure to bring to you a book of memoirs, anecdotes, and a few interesting facts and figures, that I trust will both entertain, inform and amuse.

Big Blue Sky – a celebration of the wonderful county of Norfolk!

Barrie Lawrence

Contents

Introduction

The Norfolk sky is big. And in my childhood memories, the Norfolk sky is always blue. From that big blue sky, the sun beamed gently down, filling my childhood days with benevolent light, colour and warmth. It rose early from a low eastern horizon, heralding day after day of seeming halcyon bliss, of laughter and play and family and mates, until setting late in the west behind an equally low horizon.

Under that over-arching cobalt dome, a curly-haired boy chased butterflies, rodents of various descriptions, and almost anything else that squeaked, hissed, croaked, crawled or wriggled across our varied landscape. My pleasures were simple, and they were rural. Live mice, caught bare-handed under straw bales, sat quietly in my jacket pockets as I cycled home along hedge-lined country lanes, enjoying the sweet evening air and the lowing of cattle in the water meadows beyond. And words cannot adequately express the sense of adventure, the excitement and anticipation in following coypu tracks through snow-clad pasture; an exercise that on one occasion led to a memorable conclusion. Rodents and reptiles, however, were not the only creatures chased across our Norfolk landscape; girls ('birds' to a lad in 1960s Norfolk) were pursued with enthusiasm, when time permitted. And at times, the birds chased me, which was not always the fun one might imagine.

Distant days, even viewed through rose-tinted spectacles, can be wistful indeed. For though largely carefree, there was the occasion when, following a domestic explosion, my father caught fire. Family life and childhood fun went into a muted abeyance for a period as he slowly recovered. If he really recovered. And was that childhood so untroubled when Roger the Rough pushed me over, depositing his ample aromatic frame onto my stomach until I promised to be his friend again? Schooldays were an adventure in learning and discovery, of being enthralled with conkers and marbles, but always against the background of bullying and corporal punishment. However, being put into hospital for a few days by the bully Big Ronnie and his sidekicks, and receiving a stroke of the cane for using a naughty word in the playground, pales into a relatively insignificant oblivion when compared with the near idyllic bliss of fun under that big blue sky.

Born in the county of Norfolk in 1944, I have spent most of my life within its borders. Our family enjoyed Norfolk seaside holidays in the 1950s, with buckets, spades, donkey rides and pier shows. During my lifetime, my father's car evolved from a handsome long-bonneted 1930s Riley 9 through to a relatively bland 1990s Rover 200. AA men had saluted us along the way in those early days. So much has changed.

That same sun shone on cheerful Charlie, our gardener, an unforgettable character, whose life took a most surprising turn; and it shone on Sam, the foreman, when I worked on a 1960s fruit and poultry farm. Sam had worked on a *pyghtle* and always brought his *wittals*. The broiler houses I had to clean out from time to time left my flesh creeping. I cycled to work in those days; in fact, I cycled everywhere across Norfolk's varied but distinctive landscape. Today my wife and I explore on foot, though I have been walking the county since my earliest years. And at times, even in my seventies, I find myself kicking leaves with the same carefree abandon enjoyed so long ago as a toddler.

Astride my Trent Tourer bicycle, even with my thoughts full of reptiles and rodents, I could not ignore some remarkable buildings dotted along the landscape. Norfolk's medieval churches are both commanding and beautiful, complemented by 125 round-towered Saxon churches. The construction is often of our local Norfolk flint. To me, during my childhood, church meant boredom and a never-ending succession of jumble sales. Yet that was also the prelude to a spiritual journey.

Here in Norfolk, we *do different*. Because in a rather quaint and charming way, Norfolk *is* different. The county is out on a limb, and the people are relaxed and just a little behind the times. Even more so when I was a boy, enjoying and enduring school, pursuing wildlife, engaging in *mardles*, talking *squit*, and playing in the *muck*; also, there were *shivers* in fingers. For whereas some might feel that Norfolk characters have a relatively limited vocabulary, there are within it words not recognised elsewhere. As a Norfolk lad, returning to the county in 1953 after a short spell away, I had to learn these words. So if you are visiting, or might one day holiday in Norfolk, or indeed are a relative newcomer to the county (thirty years?), let me explain.

I will also describe some of our county's landscape and features, but this is certainly not a guide book. Neither is it a history book, though I make mention in passing of some notable Norfolk individuals such as the iron-age queen Boudicca, Admiral Horatio Lord Nelson, the singing postman, and Stephen Fry. A vignette of Norfolk characters stroll across the pages, each one a part of the colourful pastiche of childhood adventures (and some a little later in life) enjoyed during nearly eighty years in this most attractive of counties. The names of a number of people in the book, especially those who talked squit, have been changed in order to save embarrassment.

It was originally intended to have a few sketches to add interest to the text, and a deal was struck with a professional artist, recommended for his work. But alas, he appeared to be suffering from artist's block, and nothing suitable arrived. And then friends and family rallied round - one daughter, three grandsons, a lady in our church, and the son of another couple. Even I had a go. We are all amateurs - and some of us more than others. So, if the little thumbnail sketches appear a trifle quirky, remember - this is Norfolk!

PH

Most of all, this book is *FUN*, as I celebrate the romance, adventure, and occasional poignancy, of a childhood, and a little later, lived in rural Norfolk. So let me introduce you to my family, friends and adventures - and all under a big blue sky.

Barrie Lawrence
Frettenham, Norfolk
January 2022

Thumbnail Sketches

Sketches supplied by family and friends as follows -

Pauline Hurrell (friend) PH
Jonathan Wilson (friend) – JW
Rachel Hodgson (daughter) – RH
Elisha Hodgson (grandson) – EH
Jonathan Hodgson (grandson) – JH
Benjamin Hodgson (grandson) – BH
Yours truly - BL

Chapter One

My Norfolk Family

Rats, Marie's cooked legs, bird nesting, shooting, cannabis....

"No!" said Brenda's father. "Quite unsuitable. Definitely No!"

Brenda had just informed her parents that she had become engaged to be married to Dick, and being under twenty-one years of age, needed their written consent in order for the marriage to proceed.

Great Britain had recently declared war on Germany, and now it seemed that her parents were doing likewise to her and fiancé Dick. No! - he was eight years older than her. No! - they had been far too hasty. No! - she was barely out of her teens. No! - his father worked on the railway. Now, *that* was probably at the heart of the matter. In short, Brenda's parents were middle-class and Dick's family were not. So No!

"If you won't give consent, then Dick and I will go away and get married on my twenty-first birthday," had been the threat. And so, in order to avoid family embarrassment, the well-to-do parents of privately educated Brenda caved in at the eleventh hour, and on 27th April 1942, six days before her twenty-first birthday, she walked down the aisle on her father's arm, married bank clerk Dick, eight years her senior and whose father worked on the railway in Bedfordshire.

They had met when working together in Barclays Bank in Cambridge. After a day or two's honeymoon, Dick returned to his regiment. These were the war years. Brenda lived with her parents over the furniture, haberdashery and drapery business in Bungay in Suffolk. Dick came home on leave for Christmas 1943. The consequence? I was born in September 1944. The county of my birth was Norfolk, as the nursing home was just over the border from Bungay. The following year, the war ended, my father came home, and resumed working as a clerk in the bank. My parents rented rooms before buying their first property, *The Retreat.* My sister Julia was born on 14th January 1947. And Norfolk, the county of my birth, became the county of my childhood. The bank moved its staff from branch to branch, but except for one short spell outside the county during infancy, my childhood years, and indeed the majority of my adult life, have been enjoyed under a Norfolk sky.

****

And so began my seventy-plus year romance with the county of my birth. Love at first sight can be deceptive, with the chemistry of the relationship, and cartwheeling hormones, blinding one to the otherwise possible incompatibility. Perhaps the companionship of toddlers seamlessly developing into childhood friendship, and later evolving into a romance of sweethearts, leading to the fulfilment and satisfaction of a lifetime marriage, has stronger foundations. And so with my love for Norfolk.

The roots of this love affair are found in the immediate post-war years. Big blue sky? Quaint coastal villages, where cottages built of local flint were the homes of warm-hearted folk? Medieval church buildings of huge proportions, with their history embedded in the past prosperity of a flourishing trade in textiles? These delights, and a thousand more, were to be discovered later, whilst in the 1940s I crawled, toddled and then walked, aware only of the immediate family, and the village in which we lived. The rest would unfold in due course.

So let me introduce my family. We are a few years on from the end of the war, and I have progressed from toddler to infant. Riding a red tricycle around the garden was exhilarating - I was a racing driver, wasn't I? - whilst baby sister Julia was either in pram, high chair or cot. My mother, Brenda, was beautiful beyond description, and that was simply a fact. I would not have described her as around five foot seven inches, slim, and with shoulder length brown hair, but others might have done so. She was more than content to be a housewife and mother, so proud of her children and very much in love with my father, Dick. But then, he *was* very special; absent all day, but quietly admired, and tremendous fun at times. Tall, fair and handsome, he enthused over sport and family. I later realised that as a young man, he had probably given preference to chasing balls in sports of all descriptions, and girls, over and above attaining academic achievement; his father had advised him that bank clerks were secure in their employment, and so that was his lifetime occupation.

****

"Which dress do you think I should wear today? You can choose, Barrie," said my mother. I was a toddler, probably of two or three years. Everybody was very tall, and I have no recollection of a sister. This must be one of my earliest memories.

3

Did I know the word 'red' at that age? Maybe not, but I knew which dress my mother should wear. She was so slim and beautiful, and surely deserved to have the frock that was in a league of its own. Like Mummy. Of the dozen or so dresses on the rail in the wardrobe, I could see only one.

"That one, Mummy," pointing to the red frock. So my mother spent the day, and many other days, dressed in scarlet; and if she did not want to do so, she did not ask me to choose which dress.

****

"Be careful!" screamed mother. And then, "Dick. *NO!*" But it was too late. My sister and I leapt for our lives as something resembling a huge, fabric-enclosed cannon ball rolled across our sitting room floor, and crashed into the armchairs. There was hysterical laughter from my mother, and Julia and I could hardly contain our mirth, as father unfolded himself. Gasping for breath and laughing heartily at the same time, he managed to say, "That's called a somersault. I used to do a lot of them when I was younger, and I thought you would like to see one." That was seventy years ago, and remains an indelible childhood memory. With father nearly forty, mother was concerned that he should be careful with himself, and being on a tight budget, careful with the furniture which they were now heaving back into position.

****

Those early memories, the days of the red frock and the fabric-enclosed cannon ball, were times of seemingly unabated happiness for my parents and me. Father drove to the bank, where he was a cashier, in his stylish Riley 9 each morning, and mother enjoyed home, toddler Barrie and baby Julia, often wearing a scarlet dress. We were unaware, of course, that a serious accident would soon change our lives forever. And there were increasing financial constraints in the background, that would from time to time cause a degree of tension during the succeeding years. However, the marriage was happy and stable, and lasted over sixty-five years until my father passed on at the age of ninety-four. And nearly all my childhood memories are happy ones, with the sun shining down from that big blue Norfolk sky.

****

What causes us to reflect upon our distant, even childhood memories? For many of us, it can be music. Hearing any of the Beatles numbers from their early years immediately takes me back to my room in a London University hall of residence in 1963. One whiff of Calor gas, and I am back in a caravan with my parents, on holiday near Great Yarmouth in the 1950s, and so on. But there are also those truly poignant moments, that deeply move one's emotions and bring the past crashing into the present.

Lightning struck twice in the same place. *Twice!*

It was 11th November 2007, and we had been in New Zealand two days, staying with family. A month was planned, and then Thailand. There was a phone call for me.

"I am really sorry Barrie, and I know you are planning to be away for a month, but father has just died back here in England," said my sister. Alongside concern for my mother, there were innumerable memories of days with my father, from earliest childhood, through to a few weeks previously. The somersault that temporarily wrecked our sitting room, bird nesting, rifle shooting together - a myriad of precious memories of father and son, bonding over many years. In fact, six and a half decades. Let me share some of those memories with you, but first...

Again lightning struck, and in the same place. *Ouch*! It was eleven years later, on 12th January 2019, and we had once more landed at Auckland airport in New Zealand. We turned our mobile phones on, and there was bleeping from around the cabin. My mobile chirped, and I opened the message that had just arrived. "I am sorry to tell you that mother has died back here in England this morning."

The words caused a well of emotion. Wendy leaned across and held my hand. Once more, I reflected over seventy years during which my mother had been an integral and much-loved part of my life, with memories stretching back to the 1940s, the immediate post-war years. There was the scarlet dress, but so much more. Mother had taught me to read from the age of three, and without that and her subsequent coaching for the eleven-plus examination, I would not have passed those academic hurdles that took me to dental school and beyond so many years later. The influence of my parents had been profound.

When my father died twelve years earlier, we had spent around four hectic days watching our three Kiwi grandchildren perform ballet, play football, and do gymnastics, whilst also cramming in restaurant, winery, and late-night conversations with my daughter and son-in-law, before cancelling everything else and flying home to look after mother. This time was different. My sister so kindly said we should continue the holiday as there was no urgency. This had also been mother's wish. "If I pass on while you are in New Zealand, like your father did, don't rush back."

My parents would never claim to approach perfection, but they were thoughtful and caring, creating a secure and loving environment and foundation for my sister and me. Norfolk family life has changed a lot over the last seventy or so years, but for me, perhaps to a small extent gazing back through rose-tinted spectacles, my childhood was one of halcyon days. Such days are gone forever, but live on in my memory. Let me tell you about some of them.

****

It was the late 1940s, and the nation was still recovering from the Second World War. Rationing had been introduced at the outbreak of war in 1939 to ensure a fair distribution of goods that became scarce, starting with petrol, but soon extending to butter, sugar and bacon. Before long eggs, milk, meat, confectionery and a whole range of goods were included. My parents had married in 1942, I was born in September 1944, and the war ended in Europe on 8th May 1945. However, rationing of some items continued until 4th July 1954.

"Come on Barrie. You can collect the eggs this morning," said mother, and we would enter the hen house, where I removed warm eggs from the nesting boxes. For my parents, the constraints of rationing were mitigated by the relief that the war was over. And by keeping poultry. From the very early days of the war, eggs had been rationed to one per adult a week. If available. And that was not lifted until 1954. So whilst townies and city dwellers endured this restriction, it was rather different for those of us residing in a rural location, such as Norfolk. In fact, mother cooked eggs for family breakfast every morning, and we enjoyed roast chicken most weekends. Additionally, and unofficially, eggs could be exchanged for other rationed goods. Our kitchen garden ensured that roast chicken was accompanied by fresh vegetables twelve months a year.

Mother gave a scream. "There's rats," she yelled. I was on the back lawn, throwing a tennis ball onto the pitched roof of the house, and watching it roll back down. How many hours a week did I spend throwing that ball up onto the tiles? And did I ever attain real ball sense? Rats - I wasn't sure what 'rats' were, but ran round to the chicken run to investigate. Mother was shaking, and shouted to our gardener, Mr. Scripts. "I've just seen two rats." He came running, spade in hand. Ready for action, he pulled his cloth cap more firmly into place, a look of firm determination and anticipated excitement on his face.

Entering the enclosed netting run, he closed the door behind him, and started making stabbing thrusts with his shovel. He grinned and muttered, "Rats! I'll get the beggars". And suddenly there were rats, careering round the run, and frantically running up the wooden posts, with Mr. Scripts jumping around with his spade. "Don't look, Barrie," said mother, pulling me away and back into the house. And before very long, a beaming gardener with a blood-spattered spade was announcing, "You won't be having any more trouble from those beggars."

The rats may have caused distress to the hens, and to mother, but I inadvertently brought near euphoric pleasure to our little egg producers. My parents were embryonic entrepreneurs in a variety of ways. Maybe something would take off and be successful; a small photography business with father carrying out his own developing, enlarging and printing, the earliest stages of a munitions company, and in the attic, spaced out along the rafters, apples and tobacco leaves. The fragrance in that loft was indescribable! And then it was decided that they would produce their own fruit wine. Beyond the lawn, the chicken house and the kitchen garden, were currant bushes galore, and of course apple trees bearing fruit destined for the rafters. My parents decided that the only suitable receptacle in which to ferment their wines would be the bread bin in the kitchen. It was a small barrel constructed of white enamel, with a tight-fitting lid. But they never told me.

Mother was busy in the garden when the baker called. I took the loaf from him, ran indoors, knowing where the bread was kept. A short while later mother returned, to be greeted with, "Mummy. There was a funny splash when I put the bread in the bin."

The loaf was well and truly infused with fermented wine. Mother pulled it into smaller pieces, and lobbed it over the netting and into the chicken run. Around fifteen minutes later, an excited curly-haired boy came running in. "Mummy. Mummy. Come and see the chickens. They keep falling over."

And if most of our food was homegrown, so was the entertainment. As soon as I was old enough to kick a football, goalposts were erected in the garden, a tennis net was stretched across the centre of the lawn, and high jump posts and bar appeared next to the orchard. Later, when we had stables in the garden at Wroxham, one was converted into a small theatre and my sister, our friends and I would give plays and shows for neighbours, who would sit on crude benches and humour us with laughter and applause. Winter time was a little more of a challenge, but in addition to father playing the circus tumbler across our sitting room floor, we played card games and board games most evenings. *Happy Families* helped us remember to say 'please' and 'thank you' in everyday life. (Older readers will understand). *Penalty* was a football card game, and *Owzthat?* was a cricket card game. My parents' enthusiasm for almost every form of sport imaginable was passed on to us through card games. This was before our first television arrived, when *Grandstand* became almost compulsory viewing every Saturday afternoon. Childhood years of bonding developed into adult years of love, respect and family cohesion. My parents read *Penguin* published crime thrillers, and listened to the wireless. Very occasionally, together with a few other children, we were taken to a house in the village where a television was flickering in the corner. We would sit on the floor and watch newsreel clips of the recent war, with Richard Burton narrating from Sir Winston Churchill's war memoirs.

"Quick. Come outside. Be quick now, Barrie. Don't miss them. Hurry, hurry...." A low rumbling sound drowned anything else mother might have said, as I ran out onto our back lawn. A formation of aeroplanes, large ones in the centre flanked by smaller craft, was slowly growling across the cloudless sky. "Bombers," shouted my mother, "and fighters. Just like in the war." I stared after them with a sense of awe, but not really comprehending their significance. On another occasion we were in the garden, when mother yelled and pointed into the sky, where a parachute was bearing a swinging pilot safely to earth, when.... *BANG*. This was three years after the war had ended, but planes occasionally had problems, and one had just crashed and exploded on the outskirts of the village where we lived.

EH

BANG! But this time it was at home, in the garage. Father caught fire, survived, but was never quite the same after this incident. His extrovert confidence had gone forever, never to return, just like the Riley 9 that had been his pride and joy until... But I will come to that in a later chapter.

Our double-fronted home, *The Retreat*, was covered in Virginia creeper; to me, it looked more special than any other house I knew. Well, more special than the other houses in the village. I was small, and to me, it was huge. And so beautiful with the creeper turning shades of rust and gold, and finally bright red in the autumn. It was some years before I learnt the word 'treat', and that confirmed my sentiments about the house being special. Treat. *Retreat*. The same... almost.

"Where are all those children going, Mummy?" One of the front rooms was designated 'Nursery'. There was a large cupboard at one end, which housed toys, such as Bagatelle (mine) and a collection of dollies (definitely not mine). The end opposite the cupboard had a sash window looking out onto the road. Mother would take me to the window and draw my attention to little boys and girls walking past, largely in twos and threes.

"They look really happy, because they are going to school," she explained. School? "To learn how to write and do sums." Write? Sums? "And to read like you do now. Only more books and stories." Mother invested time in preparing me for my first day at school. However, the best-laid plans of mice and mothers...

The day arrived. Clean shirt. Clean shoes. New pullover. Ears thoroughly washed. "You will enjoy school, and make lots of nice friends." I was one of around eight new pupils starting at the two-class village school that day. We stood in the entrance hall. Mother was confident, and proud of young Barrie. Some mothers were fussing over their children, whilst others appeared impatient to get away. A teacher appeared. "Say Goodbye to your mothers, and come with me," Miss Dellow said gently. Nobody moved, until one mother broke the silence, "Goodbye Michael. I'll come back for you later." And then, at the words, "You'll be alright," Michael let out a howl, and clung to his mother. Alarm spread like wildfire, as two or three of us shrieked, "I wanna go home." We were gently disentangled from our mothers, who were then shooed out through the door by which we had entered. But we soon settled, and if anyone did not, they were liable to find themselves standing in the corner with their hands on their head.

I treasure the memories of family life in my early years. There was no television or any other household screens, but life was a happy adventure. The quality of life was determined by the quality of people. My sister and I were blessed with parents who made time for us. They enjoyed us. When television arrived, we were included in the fun of watching comedies, and increasingly, sport. My parents always listened to us, included us, and later, father would take me rifle shooting and golfing, and mother would pore over dress designs that my sister had spent hours creating.

"Daddy. Can I play with the Meccano set please?" At that time, Meccano was a collection of metal plates, bolts and nuts with which one could build various mechanical creations. It had been invented by Frank Hornby in 1898. I think my father had always wanted a Meccano set to play with. Or maybe with which to develop his creativity? So I was given one for Christmas, and watched him produce an aeroplane, a truck, and a jeep. And sometimes I could play with it too!

He also spent hours playing with my Hornby train. Again, Hornby trains were invented by Frank Hornby. Having patented his Meccano sets, he produced the first clockwork model train in 1920. A Hornby train set was my Christmas present a year after the Meccano. And when father was at work, I played with that too!

BL

My seventh birthday was the first on which I received two identical cards. Why do I still remember that? Totally insignificant, but a quirk of childhood memory and never forgotten. A few months later, my mother would have me sit down in the dining room each morning, while she read aloud from the newspaper. Princess Elizabeth and Prince Philip were touring Africa, and then going on to Australia and New Zealand. I remember vividly the description of *Treetops*, and of the variety of wild animals the princess was viewing, and filming, from the roof. I was absolutely entranced. But it was at school that we were informed of the death of her father, King George Vl, while she was still in Kenya. Children were told to walk home slowly, and not a word was to be spoken. Silence. Respect.

****

"Her legs are *cooked*," said my father, "She's *baked* them." That was my father's answer when I asked, "Why are Aunt Marie's legs all blotchy?"

Winters could be cold and there was no central heating. We had a coal fire, and we sat close to the grate, and close to each other. As I left the fire zone to leave the room, I would encounter cold air behind the sofa, and anywhere else remote from, or shielded from, the fire. There was every encouragement to stay in that tight family group around the flames. Aunt Marie's legs were blotchy, and father said they were *cooked*. When she visited, she sat beside the fire and stuck her legs out in front of it. "She keeps the heat off the rest of us," groaned father after she had left for home at the end of a winter weekend. "She always did sit in the fiddle of the mire." My sister and I did not know what a Spoonerism was, and it was unintentional. Father was very cross about Marie having hogged the fire, and when we realised what he had said, burst out laughing until his angry stare made us stop very abruptly. "Fiddle of the mire," we would whisper to one another from time to time, and snigger quietly. Another memorable moment.

In fact, father was prone to coming out with Spoonerisms, quite unintentionally, and at times Julia and I had to leave the room for fear of collapsing with laughter and experiencing father's displeasure. Referring to another female relation, whom he found irritating, father became quite agitated, went red in the face and almost exploded with the words, "She needs a good slop around the chaps." Julia and I caught each other's eye, shook with barely-contained mirth, buried our heads in our hands, and rocketed from the room. On reaching the rear garden, we collapsed with howls of uncontrollable laughter, catching our breath and repeating to one another, 'slop around the chaps!'.

"Here. Look. A nest." And father pointed to a beautiful circular construction of twigs and moss. We were peering into the hedges along Mrs. Pigg's lane. There were speckled eggs, of blue and green hues. "Just take one egg, carefully, and the mother will return and hatch out the others." We went from nest to nest, where some eggs were turquoise, some plain blue, some olive green, and so on. Back home in the kitchen, he produced a needle, made a hole in both ends of each egg, and gently blew out the contents. Mother was concerned for the parent birds, and I was too young to consider such matters. That was the day my collection of birds' eggs started. But we had no bird books, and there was no internet. I did not know which birds were represented, and it never really grabbed my imagination. Thankfully. My father had been taught by his father, and his father before him. I taught no-one, and now it is illegal. But it was family life, father and son, bonding.

RH

No television. No computers. No electronic games. To some families today, that might sound like being trapped in a world of indescribable boredom. But during our Wroxham days, when I was around ten, my father taught me how to use a fretsaw, and I made my mother a magazine rack, and myself a toothbrush holder. (A portent of things to come?). Skills learnt in those far off years can still be applied, and today, each of my daughters has a handmade decorative musical jewelry box, and my wife has two.

Both parents loved the sea. My father's family had lived in Bedfordshire, and travelled by rail for an English seaside holiday each summer. Grandpa worked on the railway. Free rail passes took them to Eastbourne. My mother spent her childhood in Suffolk, and her family had an English seaside holiday in Devon each year. By car, because that Grandpa was comfortably off. To both of my parents, the seaside was magical, and Norfolk was surrounded by it. We had a car, and my parents rented a beach hut at Mundesley, only five miles away. We drove there at weekends. We cycled there after school on summer weekdays. I played in the sand. I swam. I loved digging deep holes until I could barely see out, even standing up. Danger? These were the 1950s. There was a fabric windshield, a mallet, a Primus stove, and deckchairs in the hut – but we often needed that windshield. A big blue sky, and yet on the beach, a whiff of the arctic.

CRUNCH! Father jumped out of the driver's seat like a Jack-in-a-box, as though he had just sat on hot coals, with an expression on his face to match. "Oh Dick, not again," sighed my mother, staring at the shattered remains of my father's plastic sunglasses lying on the driver's seat. "That's the third pair this year." Why did he leave them there, time after time, year after year? Why fall backwards into the seat like an inanimate sack of potatoes without looking first? Poor father. "Just my luck. Would you credit it?" could have been his catchphrase. My sister and I quickly suppressed our explosions of laughter. Daddy had that aggrieved look again.

****

The Norfolk Broads were on our doorstep at Wroxham, and a few miles away whilst living in North Walsham. A day boat from a boatyard in Wroxham, and the four of us would motor along the river Bure, and into Wroxham broad, and then Salhouse broad. Father would 'drive', but Julia and I would have supervised sessions at the wheel. The waters were not so busy in those days. Swans, coots, ducks and geese of all descriptions, herons, moorhen, grebes and the occasional kingfisher. There was rich and fascinating wildlife all the way. And the famous ukulele-playing George Formby's home was on the riverside.

We enjoy such times, and learn. A generation later, as a father of four young girls, I knew how to bond. We would go to the beach, and we would take boats out on the river and broads. Every weekend, I would plan one memorable activity that, as a family, we could look back on. Having fun. Bonding. Creating memories. And now my daughters are mothers, and I see them doing the same. From generation to generation, we pass on family values.

****

Sitting on the runway in Auckland, waiting whilst the jetbridge was positioned and for the invitation to disembark, took me back to that earlier holiday there, when I had received news that my father had passed on. I loved him, but the passing of many years, and my own experience of fatherhood, enhanced my appreciation of the time and energy he had invested in me. However, it was also to lead to a problem. I needed to go to the police.

I held my breath, and summoned up my courage. I had rehearsed my lines. "I have a box of live ammunition for you, officer. Wouldn't want it to fall into the wrong hands." Or maybe I should just dump it and run for my life.

PH

It was autumn 2008 and I walked into the police station and approached reception. There was no-one there, so I rang the bell. A lady police officer appeared and asked if she could help me. I told her that the box on the counter held about 25 rounds of live ammunition.

"Thank you sir," she said, picking it up and placing it under the counter.

"Would you like my name and address?" I asked.

"No need," she said. "Thank you, sir."

Perhaps I should have said, "But I'm the Jackal!", or "I'm training as a terrorist, and just have far too many boxes of ammo." Maybe she was trying to decide what to have for supper that night, or perhaps she was in love. She certainly was not interested in twenty-five rounds of live ammunition that was lethal, and almost certainly illegal. I had been clearing out my father's bureau.

My parents had moved into that house around twenty years earlier. That too was marked by the discovery of illegality.

"What's the plant over by the wall in your back garden, Dick?", a cousin had asked my father.
"No idea," he had replied. "I don't think I've had one of those before. Some sort of shrub. Interesting smell. Give it a sniff"
"It's cannabis, Dick," said a neighbour who had dropped in to wish them well. "Don't ask me how I know, but it's definitely cannabis."
"But we're right opposite the police station. Are you sure?" retorted Mother.
"Absolutely certain," replied the neighbour. "I know my plants. Well, that one I do!"

Twenty-four hours later there was a patch of bare soil by the wall, father had had a bonfire, and couldn't stop laughing, smiling, and rolling around on the ground. I jest - it's not true, but the plant had gone. And now, twenty years later, I discovered a carton of live ammunition in his desk that I was clearing out.

"How would you like to go shooting?" my father had asked me nearly half a century earlier. "There's a club on the far side of town, and a chap who comes into the bank is a member. A military man, rank of Colonel. Says he will pick us up on his way there every Thursday, and he has a Daimler. What do you think?"

It was 1961, and I was just seventeen. So we joined, and enjoyed the shooting, the coffee and biscuits, the camaraderie amongst members - and riding in the Daimler. We had to buy our own ammunition, which was .22 calibre cartridges.

"And remember to put them in the locked safe at the end of the evening Dick," said the secretary. "We don't want people taking them home and getting into trouble. It's not legal to walk around this country with live ammunition. Unless you have a licence." Perhaps my father was becoming a little forgetful - it was well over forty years later that I discovered the ammo in his desk.

Dad was a sportsman. Any sport, and he would hold his own. Or excel. He was quite a good shot, whereas I was mediocre. On a good evening. My best memory of the club was the local *Bisley*.

The headquarters of the *National Rifle Association* is at Bisley in Surrey. Nearby is the *Bisley Gun Club*, and the *Bisley Clay Pigeon Shooting Ground*. Local shooting competitions in the U.K. are called *Bisleys* because of the HQ, where the national competitions are held.

"Go on, Barrie Boy," said the secretary. "You're not the best, but it's a handicap competition. Everyone's got a chance." So father entered both of us. During the two or three weeks before the actual day, my shooting accuracy had been even worse than usual. On the day of the Bisley, I was amazing. "Looks like you've won just about everything," said the secretary. And though he could have suspected that I had rigged it with poor cards handed in, followed by some half-decent shooting on the day, he knew me too well, was good humoured, and seemed pleased for me. My name appeared in the local newspaper. And father was proud of me.

"I'm getting some new golf clubs," father told me. "So you can have my old ones, and we'll both join Mundesley Golf Club and play a round or two when we can." I never excelled, sometimes missed completely, and my father was incredibly patient. Always. Proud? "This is my boy, and he's going to be a dentist," was only surpassed a decade later, when at the end of a round, and back in the clubhouse, he would say loudly, "Meet my son Barrie. He's a dentist in Norwich, you know."

Both parents took a real interest in my career, and years later, my father would ask me how many patients, how many staff, what I enjoyed most, etc. My mother always told me that she would gladly come to the surgery and help if I was short-staffed. On a few occasions I would inform her that I was struggling because of nurses being away sick, and she would drive the twenty miles into Norwich and be waiting for me in the surgery. Staff found a white coat for her, and she would beam with excitement. If I left the surgery, I would sometimes catch her saying, "I'm his mother, you know," as I returned. I would help her select the appropriate instruments for whatever treatment I was carrying out, and she would often ask, quite loudly, "Have you got all the right tools, dear?" *Tools?* - the patient should have been alarmed. Black and Decker - open wide!

****

My parents both became committed fans of Norwich City Football Club. They loved football. When I was young, we would drive all over Norfolk to watch Bungay Town play. Grandpa had been a player, secretary, treasurer, chairman, and any other office going at the club. I would follow him like a shadow, and be at his side when he gave the team their pep talk before the match, and at half-time. He had his hands in his pockets, and so did I. He nodded, and so did I. He frowned and so did I.

Later, after Grandpa passed on, Norwich City became the team my parents followed. My father had taken me to the ground one weekday when I was quite young; he wanted me to see how big it was compared with village pitches. Many years later, my eldest daughter, aged around fifteen, took me to a match. Around us, all her friends started singing. My daughter giggled, and shouted in my ear, "Dad, would you mind putting your fingers in your ears for the fourth line."

"Hey, where's my hat? What the…?" The football incident which is most memorable was in the final minute of a very important match. The atmosphere was electric. Adrenaline was pumping through every vein, spectators, players, everyone. In the final seconds, Norwich City scored, and won. The crowd leapt to their feet, and a great cheer went up. My parents were ecstatic, when - *whoosh*! My father's hat was torn off his head by the person standing behind him, who threw it high in the air, with a great victory cheer. My father never saw that hat again. He had never been so aggrieved at seeing his team win.

****

In some homes, the advent of television had spelt the end of family conversation, card games, reading, and the enjoyment of family relationships. We enjoyed television, but still had meals in the dining room around the table and talked, and played golf and went shooting. Central heating meant we no longer needed to huddle round the fire, but we chose to be together. I am so glad that computer games had not been invented, observing so many young (and not so young) men today glued to their screens hour after hour.

Grandparents visited often, and we reciprocated. Likewise uncles, aunts and cousins, especially at Christmas and Easter. Which could be perplexing.

It was Christmas Eve, and we were staying at the home of our cousins and family in Hertfordshire. "We're putting stockings on the end of your beds, and if you wake up and open them before six o'clock, don't come through and wake us," said mother. Julia and I were bursting with anticipation. Christmas was exciting anyway, but sleeping in a room with our three cousins was *fun*. And it was Christmas! Those empty stockings might well be bulging after Santa had visited.

And then Aunt Eileen came in and spoke to our three cousins. "Here are your pillow cases. I will put them on the ends of your beds, and I don't want you running through to us with them before it is light. OK?"

Julia and I stared in near disbelief at these relatively huge sacks, and then back at our stockings, meagre by comparison. Santa Claus was a kind man, but this seemed so unfair. And if their pillow cases really got filled, then in future I would ask for one too. And so would my sister.

Morning arrived, very early, and I looked down to the foot of the bed to see a bulging stocking. And then across

23

to cousin David, in the next bed. His pillow case was so full that some presents had spilled out. It was still exciting as Julia and I opened our stockings, and experienced the wonder and awe of amazing little toys, surprises, games and chocolates. We were almost too absorbed to notice cousins tearing the wrapping off a veritable pile of major presents.

After breakfast, we were told that it was time for us to open the gifts from family members, and we adjourned to the sitting room, where Julia and I each received a pile of wrapped gifts of various sizes.

"Where are *our* presents, Mummy?" one of the cousins asked, to be told, "Santa brought yours, and you opened them in the bedroom. Now go and play while we open ours." And I suspect they might have considered putting a stocking out the following year, to see if Santa would fill it with small but wonderful gifts, prior to having family presents later.

BH

I was blessed to be part of a loving and inclusive family, where within our corporate structure and culture, I was spoilt by grandparents, whilst with cousins, we sometimes knocked the corners off one another. It gave a solid foundation for my own life, and there were great rôle models amongst my relations. Maybe I caught something of that ethos. Wendy and I have six daughters living in five different countries. We are blessed that two, and their respective families, currently live in Norfolk.

There are twenty grandchildren. We try and visit each family at least once a year. Even New Zealand - though it has not always been possible. And at our home in rural Norfolk, we slept twenty-six people and one dog Christmas 2019. Wendy and I were on the sitting room floor, and some grandchildren had mattresses on bedroom floors. We are a large family, and we love it.

I was born in Norfolk. Our children have been brought up in Norfolk, though they are now global in location. Our two eldest Dutch grandchildren from Amsterdam, were bubbling with excitement when they came to stay without their parents. They were aged four and five, and told us, "You have the best house in all the world." Because there are lots of places to hide? No. Because there are two staircases to chase up and down? No. Because there are lots of rooms to explore, and toys to enjoy? No. Why then? "Because it's *pink*, of course!" they exploded with giggles. Suffolk pink actually, but it's in Norfolk! And usually under a big blue sky.

I love this county of my birth, and my seventy-plus year romance with it continues. But in Norfolk, we 'do different', as the saying goes, and part of that is the accent, and indeed, at times the vocabulary itself. Have you ever been to a church where you sat in a poo? Have you lived in a community where a number of chaps were called Grum? Can you remember a time when you got a shiver in your finger? Have you ever interrupted a time of troshing at the pyghtle in order to partake of your wittals? I dussent even try and think of how many unique words Norfolk people use in a mardle, and to outsiders, they might sound like squit. So in the next two chapters, come with me and explore, and even learn, some of our Norfolk language and culture.

Chapter Two

Cleaning Boots

*An introduction to the Norfolk language and culture -
boots, Grum, June and June, and dwile flonking.*

Mrs. Lamb, our new char lady, cleaned boots on a
Saturday, she told us. My mother thought this sounded
both mundane, but also rather specialised; boots, rather
than shoes, or general footwear. And when she enquired
about the number of boots Mrs. Lamb cleaned on a
Saturday, was surprised to be told that she cleaned very
few; maybe six on a Saturday morning, but up to a
dozen, which could take all day. It was 1953, and we
were new to Wroxham, and on a learning curve.

Banks move their staff from branch to branch. Well, they
did so during the days of my childhood, until my father
was given a move from North Walsham, and said 'No!'
He was told that there would be no further promotion if
he stayed in one branch, and happily accepted that in
order to enjoy the town and the friends my parents had
made there, through until his retirement. But in earlier
days, he had been from branch to branch, not least in
Norwich. After a short spell out of the county during my
early childhood, my father was moved to the Wroxham
branch. There, in the village, and around one mile from
the bank itself, my parents found the house that would be
our home for the following five years. An end terrace
house at the bottom (the road sloped down) of an unmade
road, where a five-barred gate kept the rest of humanity
out of our wonderful new world. Old stables that my
friends and I would use as dens, until hired out as garages

27

or used to house my parents' hens, just oozed the invitation to adventure. As did the woods behind our property, where a few loose panels in the fence gave access to a make-believe world of cowboys and Indians, cops and robbers, or anything else we might soon be viewing on our flickering black and white television screens, and which we would enact and relive in that arboreal paradise.

Before relocating to our new home, my mother would visit the area, explore, and return with reports of what she had experienced. It sounded to my young ears as though we were moving into a new world - deepest Norfolk. "They have a very strange accent when they speak," she would tell us, and go on to relate conversations she had overheard on buses. "'Oi hev' said this girl sitting behind me, and then her friend would say, 'Noo yew ain't', and they would continue with Oi this and Oi that. I don't know if we'll be able to understand them too easily".

At the age of eight, I did not want to move to Wroxham. Later, at the age of thirteen, I did not want to move to North Walsham. Moving meant losing one's friends and having to make new ones. However, I soon became enchanted with our new home, garden, and the village in general. The accent was only strongly present in a minority of the boys and girls at school, and it was not difficult to understand. One did not take too long to tune in, so to speak.

Robert had lived in Park Road all eight years of his life, and being just a little younger than me, we became friends. Perhaps I could not understand everything he said, and maybe my mother said he was a rough lad, and smelly, and fat, but he was my friend.

We chased each other through the woods, ganged up against smaller boys, and endlessly kicked a football around the park at the top of the road, and the small patch of land my father had cleared between two of the stable buildings in our garden. But Robert was increasingly in trouble at school and in general with the residents of Park Road, and the time came when my mother laid down the law.

BH

"Your friendship with Robert must end. He is a bad influence, and I don't want you getting into the sorts of trouble that he is heading for". And so, on the way back from school the next day, I plucked up courage and told Robert that we could no longer be friends. He stared at me in a manner that was full of menace. He was short, muscular, usually sweaty, and with a hint of Mediterranean duskiness attributed to his alleged Italian prisoner-of-war father. He gave me a huge push and I found myself laying on the ground, gasping for air. And then Robert calmly plonked his generously aromatic frame upon my stomach, causing further respiratory distress. As I heaved and wheezed under his more than adequate carcass, he demanded, "Oi want yew to be moi friend, and oi'll sit on yer till yer says yis." ('I want you to be my friend, and I'll sit on you until you says yes'). I complained that I could hardly breathe, and that my mother had decreed on the matter. But Robert calmly sat on me until I eventually complied. Arriving home a little late from school, my mother stared at me in horror as I entered the house. My blazer was covered in mud, moss, dandelion seeds and assorted grasses. "What have you been doing? Where have you been?" she enquired. And I explained that I had told Robert that the friendship was over, and that he had sat on me until I had relented. And although my parents did all in their power to break the bond with Robert the Rough, living so close and being of similar age resulted in a degree of camaraderie until our family moved from the village five years later.

My sister found a friend in Martina Huson, who lived just a few doors along from Robert. Martina was a diminutive little waif, and an only child. Her parents struggled to make ends meet, but young Martina was their pride and joy, and their catchphrase was, "She ain't 'arf li'ell, but she gart a big brine". And just in case that is in any way obscure, they were saying, "She isn't half little, but she's got a big brain." I was to hear my parents repeat that, grinning at each other, many times and in many situations for years to come.

And next door to the Husons was the Lamb family. Thin, wiry, Kenneth Lamb, was a builder's labourer, loving husband, devoted father, and committed Norwich City football fan. Sylvia was the elder of the two daughters, and was relatively plain, whereas young Lulu (real name Lucy) was slim, glamorous, mini-skirted, and caused immense irritation to my mother. "I wouldn't stand for that in a daughter of mine," she would repeatedly exclaim. There was real passion in her voice - but I think my father finding Lulu quite something to behold, influenced mother's attitude on such matters.

"Oi clean boots evry Sa'urday", Mrs. Lamb volunteered. "Hev done for yairs". Which led my mother to ask how many? Where? Whose are they? And the answers enlightened us to the way in which the lives of so many people in the region were influenced strongly by the broads - the man-made lakes, centuries old, and now a centre of tourism.

"Boots. Oi clean all sorts of boots. Mainly Oi clean crooser boots, but there is also sailin' boots and 'ouse boots. They're all boots, and all need a clean on Saturdays. So I might jist clean up to eight boots on a Saturday. And oonly in the summer, during the arlidays." So now we knew. And we were coming to realise that in Norfolk, people *do different*, as the saying goes.

Furthermore, Mrs. Lamb used a dwile in her work. That I shall return to at the end of this chapter.

****

I was thirteen, and although I had said Goodbye to so many friends in Wroxham, I was starting to get to know lads in the town of North Walsham, where we now lived. We overlooked the playing fields of the Paston School, and it was to this establishment that I trudged, briefcase in hand, every morning and afternoon.

"Wotcher, John," I'd greet several of my friends, John being the most common boy's name in our school. "Wotcher Barrie," they would reply, as 'Wotcher' was the usual greeting we used then. I rarely hear the word used today, as it has been superseded largely by 'Are yer awlroight?' ('Are you alright?'). Yes, that is a greeting in Norfolk.

Boy's names. There must be hundreds; and even back in the late 1950s in rural Norfolk, where no-one of any ethnicity other than white Caucasian was to be seen, there was a huge number of different names. Those were the days when Johns and Davids were two a penny, and one knew several chaps called David John (though none called John David). Peter, Chris and James were common, and though very few were called Thomas or William, my father's generation was rife with them (with most William's being called 'Bill'), and there was to be an explosion of them two decades later. And there were few Kevins or Scotts in those days, and in my circle of friends, no Dominics, Ruperts, Gustavs or Barnabys.

And I had never met a boy called Grum. Until...

"Wotcher Barrie. Meet Grum", said my school friend Andrew. "Grum, this is Barrie. He's fairly new to the town. Lives up Station Road, overlooking the playing field. He wants to be a dentist one day, but he's not a bad chap."
"Wotcher Grum," I greeted my new acquaintance. Momentarily, there was just the shadow of a question on Grum's face. Grum lived on a large estate on the far side of town, and I wondered whether there were other Grums in that neck of the woods.

And there were. Over the following few months I met, perhaps, two or three other lads called Grum. They were decent friendly chaps, and all came from the same area of town. Strange, I thought. And when greeted with a 'Wotcher Grum', they would usually pause for just a fraction of a second. Just momentarily, but a definite pause, a something, a blankness in the eyes that was immediately gone again.

And then all was made clear. It was time for my six-monthly dental examination, and I duly turned up at Sandy Pitts Steele's surgery.

Sandy (real name Charles) was an inspiration, and one of the reasons I became a dentist myself. Orange silk shirt, huge gold medallion round his neck swinging from side to side, pink trousers, loud, using strong language, and courting a glamorous girl still in the sixth form at the girls' high school, Sandy was a legend in his own lifetime. Today he would be struck off.

RH

I took a seat in the waiting room, dreading the probe that would run over every surface of every tooth in my mouth, but looking forward to two minutes of conversation with the local celebrity. And in walked Grum. Which Grum? The first Grum, that I had been introduced to by Andrew my first week or so in town. "Wotcher Barrie," he gasped. "I was almost late. Had to run all the way here."

He had hardly sat down when the door from the surgery opened, and Sandy's mini-skirted dolly bird of a nurse beamed round the room, and called, "Graham Godfrey". Up jumped Grum, and... But wait, the nurse had called 'Graham', and so why had Grum...?

There are times when I consider myself slow. Grum was never a Norfolk name; it was a Norfolk pronunciation. Grum was Graham, and all the other Grums were Grahams. Their parents called them Grum, and their mates called them Grum, but the dentist called them Graham. And when I greeted them with "Wotcher Grum", it did not sound quite right to them, and although

33

they were not sure what was wrong, they knew it was wrong. Maybe it sounded wrong because I had not developed a consistent Norfolk accent in all that I said at that time. So, after the enlightenment in the dentist's waiting room, I called Grum Graham, and all other Grums Graham.

Then there was the local saddler whose shop was in Vicarage Road. His name was Mr. Hurt. Well, most people called him Mr. Hurt. And then I discovered that the dentist called him Mr. Hewitt. And just maybe, perhaps, his name was actually Grum Hurt. Or indeed, if the dentist called him Stuart Hewitt, he would have been Sturt Hurt. Norfolk!

A character who made our accent known nationally was Allan Smethurst, a postman. He recorded a song that he had penned himself, *Hev Yew Gotta Loight Boy?* Born in Lancashire, he spent most of his childhood in Sheringham in North Norfolk. Later, on his post rounds, he hummed and sang songs he had composed himself, all in the Norfolk dialect. He recorded *Hev Yew Gotta Loight Boy?* and after it was aired on *Radio Norfolk*, his recording became a best seller. He went on to make an appearance on *Top of the Pops*, receive an *Ivor Novello award*, and perform in the summer season of 1965 at the *Windmill Theatre* in Great Yarmouth. Known nationally as the *Singing Postman*, Allan put Norfolk on the map.

Norfolk turkeys were made legendary by Bernard Matthews - and once again, so was the Norfolk dialect. As a young man, he bought 20 fresh turkey eggs for one shilling each, and a paraffin fuelled incubator. But he failed to budget for feeding them. A few years later, in 1950, he started again by buying turkeys and housing them in a thirty-five bedroomed mansion, Great

Witchingham Hall. He and his wife lived in two unheated rooms, while turkeys were hatched in the dining room, reared in the Jacobean bedrooms, and slaughtered in the kitchen. The business took off, not least due to the memorable commercials on national television, where Bernard Matthews described his turkey meat as *bootiful*. This is probably the outstanding feature of the Norfolk dialect, leading to shoppers standing in quoos, motorists filling their vehicles with fool, and church goers sitting in poos. In fact, regular church goers often sit in their own poos.

JW

I remember there being a new boy at school. It was the fifth form, and we were aged around sixteen. Ray had arrived from Birmingham, as his father's work had brought the family to Norfolk. We were amused when he told us that he came from *Brum*, and had a style of speaking that became a source of mirth to some locals. But he was very mature, and told us, "You think your girls around here are bootiful? Well, that's exactly what I think too!" He walked away laughing his head off, while the local lads stared at each other, totally bewildered.

****

Jackie was a local lady, and always had been. Narwich, as she pronounced it, had been her home from birth. My wife had met her at a ladies fellowship while we were living in the city, and as a result we were both invited to a social event at the local Methodist church where Jackie was a member.

An invitation to a tea party at Buckingham Palace would bring a certain degree of excitement and anticipation to most people. However, that would not compare with the state of near delirium emanating from Jackie, as she beamed at one person after another, gyrating around the church hall. Her heavy court shoes tended to clonk on the wooden floor as they carried her sturdy frame from one small group to another. Her hair had been in curlers, and she had clearly spent some time in front of the mirror applying make-up before arriving at the Methodist bunfight. I suspected that she had been waiting for my wife and I, for within seconds of us entering, there was a rapid clonking as she rattled over to us. "Thank yew for carmin' this ev'ning," she gushed. "There's tea, carffee and sorft drinks. And quiche. We always hev quiche at our soocials. I'm sure yew loike quiche. There's two diff'rent ones. Yew can choose, actually." And then with a giggle, "Or yew can hev one of each." Her excitement simply overflowed, and I must confess to feeling totally underwhelmed. Well really, soft drinks and *two* different flavours of quiche!

And then she was fetching two ladies over to meet us. Quivering with unabated excitement, she thrust them forward, saying by way of introduction, "This is June, and this is June."

"Nice to meet you June," I said, reaching out to shake hands with the first June. And as I shook hands with the second June, my wife echoed, "Lovely to meet you June." At which point there was the hint of misunderstanding, as Jackie's beaming smile faded momentarily. "No. This is June. That is *June*."

Jackie's explanation of a seemingly non-existent problem left me perplexed. "You are both called June?" I ventured. "No," said Jackie, now a little agitated. "This is June, and *this* is June. *June!*"

BL

We paused. We quietly racked our brains. We prayed. And suddenly, all was clear.

Jackie was not saying, 'This is June, and this is June.' She was actually saying, 'This is June, and this is Joon'. Subtle. This was Norfolk, where beautiful is bootiful, queue is koo, and Susan is Soosan. Indeed, our good friend John Pugh, respected barrister, is unfortunately addressed as Mr. Poo. Needless to say, Joan was Joon, sounding like June.
"Sorry," I said. "My mistake. Nice to meet you June. And my pleasure entirely Joan."
"That's what Oi said," Jackie added defensively, "June and *June*".

It can be a little *confoosing*, even to a chap who has been in the county for quite a while. One needs to remember that in Norfolk, we indeed *do different.*

****

The Old Vicarage Nursing Home at Little Walsingham was part of the Sue Ryder group of care centres. They employed qualified nursing staff, and additionally, recruited local people as carers. Plus the odd handyman and gardener. They also employed my wife, Wendy, herself a qualified nurse, as manager.

The village of Little Walsingham in North Norfolk is considerably larger than the nearby hamlet of Great Walsingham. This is Norfolk, though. And Little Walsingham is also regarded by many as the holiest village in England. Why? Legend has it that in 1061, the widow of the lord of the manor of Walsingham Parva had a vision of the Virgin Mary, and on three occasions. She was taken to Nazareth and shown the house where the angel Gabriel had first appeared to Mary. Back in Walsingham, the widow, whose name was Richeldis, decided to build a wooden replica of the Nazareth house that she had seen in the vision, and having failed because of the dampness of the land, awoke one morning to discover the house fully constructed and upon dry firm land. That is the story. Pilgrims have streamed to Little Walsingham over the centuries, accounting for the growth of the village. Currently around 250,000 visit the shrine every year.

Tracey, one of the carers employed at the home decided to use her holiday to travel. To see the world outside Norfolk, and especially outside of Little Walsingham. She would go for a weekend, and her destination was to be Cambridge. Her excitement was almost tangible, and she talked of nothing else. A few of the older carers, who were in their late twenties and worldly-wise, decided to have a joke at Tracey's expense.

"Hev yew gart a parsport yit?" they enquired of Tracey. The unsuspecting lass blinked, and admitted that she had not thought the excursion through as yet. But she naïvely thanked them for alerting her, leaving the ladies debating who would explain to Tracey that it was only 'for a bit of a larf' that they had suggested it. But no-one told Tracey, who became the proud owner of a passport.

The county is opening up these days, with dual-carriageway from Norwich right down to the M25 and beyond. Heading west or north-west is a different matter, with convoys of vehicles snaking along single-carriage roads, headed up by some huge piece of agricultural paraphernalia driven by a plump, rosy-faced yokel, possibly chewing straw. But when I was a Norfolk lad, the county was much more parochial. Many people who lived in North Walsham had hardly been more than a few miles from the town. If they had, it was probably to Great Yarmouth or Cromer, to walk along the promenade and consume fish and chips, served in a recent copy of the *Daily Mirror*.

Roger and Frank lived on the same housing estate, had been mates throughout their schooldays, and now worked on farms. Different farms, but similar work. They used to meet up out of school, in the coffee bar. But these days, after work, they met up over a pint at *The Bluebell*. They were content with their lot in life, but now there was television, they, like so many other Norfolk folk, were realising that there was a bigger, brighter world out there. And the jewel in the crown was London.

If you spend all your days, from birth to early twenties, say, in a rural town with a population of four or five thousand, it is difficult to appreciate the experience of being in a metropolis such as London. It was true that many people in North Walsham visited our nearest city of Norwich periodically. Most of them were familiar with the route from Norwich Thorpe station to Carrow Road, and back again. (Carrow Road is the site of the football ground where the Canaries play their home matches). Others knew the route to the colourful outdoor market where you could buy almost *anything*. And that included innumerable stalls selling fish and chips. But

Roger and Frank had set their hearts on London, which was to prove different – and challenging.

The root of the problem was that circumstances dictated that they travelled to London on different trains at different times. These two young men, and their renowned day out in London, were quite a talking point amongst some of my friends. But why did they go on different trains? However, let's move on to the day itself. The big question had been what they should do in London, and the answer was to explore and see if they could find Buckingham Palace. And a question of lesser importance, was where to meet up, and the answer was 'outside the Post Office'. It was so simple. People travelling in to North Walsham from the surrounding villages would meet 'outside the Post Office'. And those travelling to the city of Norwich would meet up 'outside the Post Office'. That's what we did in those days. And so Roger travelled to London, disembarked at Liverpool Street station, and set off looking for the Post Office. 'I wonder where the post office is in London?' he thought, still in awe of the grandeur and sheer size of the station he had arrived at. 'Cor, it ain't loike Narwich,' he thought. He walked for some time before asking directions, and finding a building with Post Office over the door, checked his watch and waited.

BH

Likewise Frank, who also alighted at Liverpool Street station, walked the streets for a while, asked directions and found himself outside a Post Office. Sadly, it turned out to be a wasted day, and back at *The Bluebell* the following evening, they had wise words for any others planning a trip to London.

"If yew dew plan to goo up London, yew oughta knoo this. There be two p'st offices in London, so if that's where yew gonna meet, make yew sure yew b'th git the same one."

****

And now back to Mrs. Lamb, who used to clean our home once a week, back in the early 1950s. She was our char lady, and she used a *dwile*. Or dwyle, as some people spell it. Indeed, it was only recently that friends Mike and Pauline, who were with us for lunch, mentioned using a dwile. Well, not Mike; but Pauline told me that she uses a dwile when cleaning her home, and always has. She is Norfolk, of course. Fred and Angie, also present, and who are relatively new to Norfolk (twenty years, perhaps), asked, "What's a dwile?"

A dwile is a floor cloth, or can be a dish cloth, and has been an integral part of the Norfolk vocabulary for generations. It is almost certainly derived from the Dutch word *dweil*, meaning floor cloth. In my later childhood, the word gained some prominence within East Anglia due to the pub game of dwile flonking. It was presented as a medieval game traditionally played by yokels, but in fact the first recorded game took place in the 1960s. Although that was described as the *revival* of dwile flonking, there is no previous record. Anywhere. Ever.

In Ludham, a Norfolk village on the river Ant in Broadland, a game of dwile flonking was banned under health and safety regulations, because of the 'speed drinking' of ale, with its inherent dangers. That was in 2010 and was reported in the national press. So let me explain the rules of dwile flonking, and the nature of the game.

Flonk. This is said to be an old English word for ale. Personally, I believe this is about as authentic as the medieval origins of the game itself. Even if it rhymes with plonk.

The game usually takes place in a beer garden, and involves two teams of twelve, often dressed as yokels. One team are *girters* and form a circle. In the middle of the circle is a chamber pot filled with ale, in which floats a dwile. The other team are called *flonkers*, and their first man steps into the centre of the circle, holding a small rod called a *driveller*. The flonker uses his driveller to pull the dwile out of the chamber pot, and while the girters dance in an anti-clockwise direction, the flonker dances round the chamber pot in a clockwise direction. The flonker then throws the ale-soaked dwile at the girters, trying to hit one on the head. If he is successful in hitting a *girter's* head, this is called a *wanton* and scores three points. Hitting the chest is a *morther* and scores two points, a hit below the belt is a *ripper* which scores one point, and a miss is known as a *swodger,* scoring no points.

If the flonker scores a swodger, the girters form a line, and the flonker has to down a pint of ale faster than the girters can pass the dwile from one end of the line to the other. This is the reason health and safety officials banned the game taking place at Ludham. Inebriation tends to be a characteristic of dwile flonking. If the flonker fails to drink all the ale, the next flonker goes to the middle, but if the flonker scoring the swodger succeeds, he goes back to the centre and throws another dwile - and might soon be drinking another pint of ale. Fast! The team with the greater number of points wins.

There are other rural East Anglian absurdities associated with the game. The referee is called a *jobanowl* and should be a *dull-witted person*. The two teams toss a sugar beet to decide which will go first, and the game starts when the jobanowl shouts, *"Here y'go t'gither."*

Advertising that there will be dwile flonking at a tavern can draw a crowd, as well as ensure good sales. It is, therefore, a popular game, these days.

We might be a little bit pecooliar – but I do love my home county.

BL

Chapter Three

A Shiver in My Finger

Further exploration of the Norfolk language - mardle, squit, shiver, shew, dussent, bishy barnabee, pyghtle, wittals, trosh, marb.

Iain and his family arrived in Norfolk from their previous home, well to the west of the country. Teaching French at the local high school was not without its challenges - and also its mysteries.

"Please sir, I've got a shiver," complained young William. He certainly appeared to be in a degree of discomfort, his shock of brown hair hanging down onto his spectacles as he fidgeted around on his chair.
"Then close the window, or go and sit by the radiator for a while," Iain suggested.
"I'll try sir," said William. "But I don't think it will help. The shiver is in my finger."

Iain stared blankly at the lad, who stared equally blankly back at Ian. There appeared to be a breakdown in communication.

****

A language, such as English, is both spoken and written. An accent, or dialect, is only spoken. However, in Norfolk...

We might say 'Oi', but we will write 'I'. We might write 'beautiful', but we may well say 'bootiful'. Yet our

45

county has words of its own, which are virtually peculiar to Norfolk. Where else in the U.K. do people stop for a *mardle*? And then again, we use words from our common English language, but with a meaning that is only understood within our county boundaries. Nowhere else in the British Isles would someone complain, "I have a shiver in my finger".

My friend Iain, the French teacher at the high school, considered the situation.

"In your finger?" he enquired.
"Yes sir. I can show you if you like. It's only a small shiver though," William added.

And all was made clear as the boy popped his finger under Iain's nose, where he clearly saw a splinter.

"Oh. You mean the splinter?"
"Yes sir. If that's what you call it. It's a shiver."

And closing the window, or sitting near a radiator, would be of no use whatsoever, which had left William perplexed. You really need a needle and tweezers to get rid of that sort of shiver.

And so let me take you through some aspects of *talking Norfolk*. Some of these stories are from my childhood, and one or two are from more mature years.

****

I had been born in Ditchingham, which lies on the very southern border of Norfolk. But in 1953, our family had been moved by the bank to the village of Wroxham. It was not exactly deepest Norfolk, but we had enjoyed a spell outside the county, again due to father's work, and we now had a little adjusting and learning ahead of us. My sister and I walked the four hundred yards or so to Wroxham County Primary School each day, accompanied by mother for the first year or so. I enjoyed school, where we were taught reading and writing, which I enthused over, almost as much as playtime. My mother had introduced me to reading from the age of around three, and books were fun. I loved the stories we read together, graduating from Book 1 to Book 2, and through to Book 12. Achievement. Just give me more books, I thought.

I was at that primary school from 1953 to 1956, and today, on a book shelf in my study, I still have a small volume, *Collins English Gem Dictionary*, a memento of those early schooldays. Inside the front cover it has the words, 'Given by the Chairman of the School Managers (Mr. E. W. Willis) to Barrie Lawrence for an essay on "Wroxham"'. Sadly, they did not include the date, but my guess would be 1955.

It was at the same school that I first heard the expression, 'You'll *get wrong*'. Within both the school I attended, and the community in which I lived, people *got wrong*. If you did not stand up when the teacher entered the classroom, you got wrong. If you could not read simple passages, or spell simple words, you got wrong. However, if you were sent to the headmaster to be punished, the expression would be inappropriate. In adult life, if your car (and most people did not own a car in the mid 1950s) was parked badly, you might get wrong with the police. But if you were caught stealing and taken to court, saying that you got wrong would be an understatement. So if you were told off, warned about poor behaviour, or scolded, you got wrong. But if there was more than a warning, the expression would be inappropriate, and stronger words would be used. "He's in roight trouble, he is. Cor blust (Blast!), he's for it".

The phrase persists. The people who *get wrong* in Norfolk are usually children, and generally those from households where the parents had *got wrong* in their childhood. Managerial and professionals, however, do not use that expression, and neither do they themselves get wrong, though they might get into trouble. Except Toby Lewis. He was probably our favourite patient at my county dental practice. He lived over forty miles away, and yet he regularly and faithfully attended every six months. Or more often, if necessary. And with unforgettable humour. The very epitome of modesty, Toby had been a patient for some years before it leaked out that he was professor of statistics at the University of East Anglia, and had authored a textbook on the subject, which was used internationally. Once when Toby came through to the surgery, it was apparent that the nurse had brought the wrong patient records with her; they were of another patient surnamed Lewis. Toby realised, beamed at us, his eyes twinkling with mischievous fun, as he chuckled, "She'll get wrong, she will. She'll get wrong." Toby and I would enjoy a good *mardle* whenever he came to the surgery, and it was he who seriously encouraged me, "Write a book, Barrie. Write a book". He echoed the comments of diners where I was a regular speaker at ladies luncheon clubs and even formal dinners of one of our two main political parties. "You should write a book, you should". They could have threatened, "And if you don't, you'll get wrong".

And supposing you did get wrong, then it was possible that someone else would tell you, "That'll larn yew".

(That will learn you). Which means, of course, 'That will teach you a lesson'.

****

"It's a bishy barnabee," exclaimed Sylvia, staring at a small creature that was moving slowly up the inside of the window. Our classes at primary school were mixed, and Sylvia was a small red-haired pudding of a girl. With freckles, of course. Blinking at the morning sun coming in through the glass, she seemed bewitched by the little creature, oblivious to the fact that Mrs. Shreeve had just entered. The rest of the class stood to their feet, as children did when their teacher entered the classroom in those days. But Sylvia remained entranced, oblivious to all else.

"Yew are a pri''y li''le creature," she muttered, and ran her finger gently along the glass, in front of the bishy barnabee. "Come to Sylvia. Oi woont hart yew". (I won't hurt you).

Bishy barnabee is an expression used exclusively in East Anglia. Or should I say 'was', as from the year 2018, it has been included in the Oxford English Dictionary. So maybe in other, more remote parts of the UK one will overhear conversations that include the words bishy barnabee. *Bishy barnabee?* It's the Norfolk name for a ladybird (the U.K.) or a ladybug (North America, Australia, New Zealand).

JW

The origin of the name is uncertain, although it is usually attributed to Bishop Edmund 'Bloody' Bonner, one-time

49

vicar in the Norfolk town of East Dereham, and later bishop of London. He lived 1500 to 1569, and became bishop of London in 1539. Legend has it that he wore a red, spotted cloak, though the authenticity of the story is contested. Interestingly, ladybird refers to the Virgin Mary.

****

Long before I understood such festivals, my parents would celebrate New Year's Eve, clinking glasses at midnight, or in their case, probably cups of tea at ten o'clock, and wishing each other 'Happy New Year'. In fact, much the same was happening across the rest of the world, starting from the International Date Line and travelling west. Except in Norfolk, for whereas everyone else refers to New Year's Eve, we celebrate Old Year's Night. (Unless, like my parents, one's background is Suffolk, or Bedfordshire, or almost anywhere else on the face of the earth.) Having spent five years in London training to be a dental surgeon, and five years in practice in Dorset in the south-west of England, something sounded vaguely wrong when, having returned to the county of my birth, I was invited to an Old Year's Night party.

BL

It was certainly going to be the old year's night, but something bugged me about it. And then, as the critical second approached, the television was switched on for the countdown, and there, across the bottom of the screen, were the words New Year's Eve. Without thinking properly (and who does at one minute to midnight on the thirty-first of December?), I blurted out, "Look. New Year's Eve. That's what it is. Not Old Year's Night", only to be corrected, "Cors it ain't. It's Old Yair's Noight. W'll blust, they gart it wrarng on the telly!" (Phonetic translation unnecessary). On a Norfolk telly? – of course it was wrong.

****

It was early summer 1963, and having completed my Advanced Level GCE examinations, which I needed to pass in order to go to London University to study dentistry, I decided to earn a little money which could be useful in supplementing my anticipated grant. At school, we were told that the summer term would not finish for another three weeks, and we were expected to attend (and twiddle our thumbs?) during that time. Or we might receive an unfavourable report. So let them, most of us decided.

I would jump on my bicycle at the crack of dawn, and pedal seven miles to the farm where I initially picked fruit, which was weighed by the punnet, and for which I received cash payment. Piece work. It was whilst cycling home one evening during the second week that I recognised the history master, Mr. Lamb, nicknamed Charlie after the 18th century essayist Charles Lamb, driving towards me on his way home. Recalling the 'unfavourable report' threat, and deciding to play safe, I swerved through an open gateway and crashed into a field of ripening barley. With the wisdom of hindsight, I expect Charlie smiled and said to himself, "Lawrence B R, trying to earn a few bob for the summer. Good luck to him!"

After three or four weeks, I was asked whether I would like to join the team that was paid hourly, and who had more job security. Just for the summer. You bet. And so I was weighing other people's punnets, and later their sacks of broad beans, and later still, pruning raspberry canes, grading bulbs, and cleaning out broiler houses. (A broiler house was used for rearing chickens for meat, and was perhaps eighty feet long and fifteen feet wide, with straw a foot or two deep. The previous inhabitants had been sent for slaughter by the time we were asked to clean them. The air was heavy with the pungent reek of ammonia, and dust reduced visibility to a few yards. We would stumble over the bodies of chickens which had been trampled, or fatally attacked by fellow residents, or simply been too weak or sick. And no-one wore a mask). After cycling the seven miles home, I would fill the bath, climb in, submerge, and then resurface and look round to see what insects, bugs, creepies, etc. might be struggling or swimming alongside me in the water.

"Hev yer brought yer *wittals*?" said Sam, the man who oversaw and instructed us. I was not sure whether I had or not. That depended on what they were. I enquired.

"Yer lunch, of course," he replied. "Wittals". Of course.

Victuals, pronounced vittles, is an archaic word of Anglo-French origin used prior to the 16th century, and in its corrupted form, continues in Norfolk.

"I couldn't git threw the day withart me wittals," said Sam. "Used to work on a pyghtle afore I come hair. And always took me wittals."

Pyghtle. Another archaic word still used in East Anglia, referring to a plot of land, and usually in an agricultural

52

context. One alternative spelling is pighill, which again suggests a farming context, in this case livestock. Another interesting explanation is that there was a time when agricultural land was of irregular shape. With increasing mechanization on farms, the fields were redesigned and became more regular, approaching squares and rectangles. The small areas of land removed from the main field were referred to as tailings, and in Norfolk, pigtails, which became corrupted to pyghtle. And so, in the Norfolk town of Aylsham, where I had my county practice for over twenty years, there is a residential road called Mill Pightle. The parcel of land was the property of the adjacent mill. In the nearby village of Trunch we find Pyghtle Close, and *The Pyghtle* is a guest house in the village of Ranworth.

****

It was a relation, of sorts. I will name no names, and keep my head down. I was walking around the garden with her (there's a clue) and we were standing under the large tree towards the top of the main lawn.

PH

"This oak tree is probably hundreds of years old," I remarked.
"That's not an oak tree," came the reply. "It's an acorn tree." And oak was pronounced *ook*, of course. We are in deepest Norfolk.
"It's oak," I said, without pausing and counting to ten, as would have been prudent.
"That's no oak tree." There was passion, because she *knew* she was right. "It's an *acorn* tree." And then she delivered the *coup de grace* with, "Look on the ground.

53

They're acorns from the tree, they are. See! It's an acorn tree."

My relation was quite local, and knew a thing or two about the world around us. Since childhood she had known what acorns were, and that they came from acorn trees. She might have heard about oak trees, but we were not talking about oak trees. We were talking about the big tree at the top of my garden, and she was identifying it for me.

PH

And here we can introduce a little more of the Norfolk language, as the lady just mentioned, and I, were having a *mardle* (a chat, a discussion), and she thought I was talking a whole lot of *squit* (nonsense), though it was possible that she might have thought to herself, 'I *dussent* (dare not) argue with him because it is *his* acorn tree'. In fact, after I *shew* (showed) her the tree, she *shew* (showed) me the acorns, and that proved what the tree was. She might have said, "*Hold yew haard*," ('hold you hard', meaning, 'please pause for a moment'), but she was *troshing* away (going full pelt and not going to stop). Now, if I had told her she was silly and ignorant, and had kept insisting that it was an oak tree, she might have told people I had been *marbbing* (mobbing - relentlessly and persistently criticizing or correcting) her. So there we have a little more of the Norfolk language, in addition to the local accent.

Shew. I have not heard people use the word shew instead of showed anywhere except Norfolk, though when I first heard it, there was a vague familiarity about it. The reason for this was the King James, or Authorised Version, of the Bible. That translation is in a form of Elizabethan English. In the early 17th century, the past tense of show was written *shew*, and during my childhood, the King James Version of the Bible was the main one used. Other, more popular modern versions, which abound today, had not been produced at that time. At school, we had a Bible reading in assembly every morning, and from time to time used our Bibles in class. It was compulsory for each pupil to possess a Bible and to have it with him at school. However, although the word shew occurs there, it was not, and should not, be pronounced 'shoe'; the pronunciation is still *show*. Unless you are in Norfolk, maybe.

****

"Your father is using manure to fix the new fence around our garden," I informed my wife, with an incredulous shrug of my shoulders.
"He's *what?*" she almost exploded.

For some years I had lived alone in a small cottage on the outskirts of the Norfolk village of Frettenham. (The village name is a corruption of *Freyden*, a Viking who settled in this area. The village wrought iron sign has a Viking longboat, paying tribute to the community's Scandinavian origins, alongside a mill and a plough). It was over thirty-eight years ago now when I bought the property, and I thank God every day for providing me with a beautiful home, opposite wooded land and looking out across fields to a mill. For at least thirty of those years the summer view from my bedroom window has been barley - a beautiful golden carpet sweeping away to the hedged horizon with well-spaced mature oak trees. One year was oil-seed rape, which was brilliant yellow.

55

Another was potatoes, and a dull purple. Broad beans were a patchy green, and 'laid aside' was largely dogs and their owners. Last year was maize, standing around ten feet in height, swaying wildly in late summer gales, and awaiting harvest. (There is a variety of maize which grows to forty-three feet in height. Now that would have put our village on the map). But most years, the view is golden.

I had been living here for just over three years when I married. We grew vegetables, but we never got to enjoy them. Rabbits did. Pheasants did. Deer did. And so it was either protect the garden, or stop growing vegetables. Or continue to help the wildlife of Norfolk become fat at our expense.

BL

"Don't you worry," said Peter, my father-in-law. "I'll put a fence up, and dig it in, and you won't get no more rabbits and creatures eating your veg." My parents-in-law were Norfolk through and through, but if I were to write his words phonetically, you might think that he came from a faraway land, or belonged to one of the county's ever-increasing ethnic minorities. And so I will continue in comprehensible English. But you get the picture. And I must also add that my parents-in-law were lovely people, the salt of the earth. Ah, *earth*. Which brings me back to Peter's fencing.

I had driven back from my county practice (at that time I had a city practice seven and a half miles to the south of my home, and a county practice seven and a half miles to the north. It was my professional heyday, with five surgeries at the city practice, and two at my county practice. I am not sure how many dentists and staff I employed, but we looked after tens of thousands of patients. And hundreds of thousands of teeth).

JH

Peter was working close to the gate through which I entered from the lane. I stopped, opened the car window and asked how he was getting on.

"I'm sticking the posts in the muck, and putting the netting on later," he informed me with a cheery smile. Muck? Why was he using that filthy stuff, and where had he obtained it? Surely the stench would be indescribable?

And so I stood in the kitchen, explaining to my wife that her father was using manure, all round the garden, and surely there would be an awful stench for months.

"What did he say exactly?" she enquired.
"He said, 'I'm sticking the posts in the muck, and will put the netting on later'. I didn't stop to watch. Or sniff. Just carried on down the drive," I explained.

There was a peal of laughter. "Muck!" she said laughing. "He's putting them in the muck! That's not manure. He's just sticking them in the ground. That's what my father calls soil. Muck is earth, or soil. Not manure."
"So what does he call manure?" I asked.
Another peal of laughter.
"What do you *think* he calls manure?" She was almost crying with laughter now. "And you thought he was pushing the fence poles in with.... manure!"

That was many years ago, and Peter has long since passed away. Mother-in-law is in residential care, and my wife started a new life with a new husband on the other side of the Atlantic Ocean.

I continue to be a blessed man, and especially since Wendy came into my life nearly twenty years ago. And sometimes, when we are working together in the garden, and especially if thinning out overgrown hedging, we will come across rotten fence posts, and netting half buried in... well, in memory of Peter for whom I had more respect than he realised, *muck*.

PH

And vegetables? I grassed over the vegetable garden around thirty years ago. Wendy now grows tomatoes, cucumbers, peppers and chillies in the greenhouse, and there is a large vine, under netting when carrying fruit. Next year we plan to produce *Chateau Lawrence*. In a tub on the patio, she grows strawberries. The expectation was that we would enjoy them in the summer, but that was not to be. Squirrels enjoy them before they are ripe, picking them whilst still green, and perching on our patio table, blatantly scoff them while we watch from the window.

Shivers, mardles, squit; and squirrels, rabbits, pheasants, deer and *muck* - I do love Norfolk.

JW

Chapter Four

Schooldays

*Billy Jones gets spanked, a military tradition, Snowball,
and Horatio Nelson.*

"Billy Jones has been a really naughty boy," said
headmistress, Miss Sandall, in front of the gathered
assembly of the whole school. "Come to me Billy," she
snapped, and the forlorn looking creature ambled
hesitantly to the front. There was a most dreadful silence,
such as might have occurred when the condemned man
was brought out for public execution in days of yore.
"This is what happens to naughty children here," she said
more calmly, and yanking Billy by the scruff of the neck,
pulled him over her knee, and walloped him time and
time again on his bottom. Overcome with shame, and
with his face red and puffy, Billy was sent back to his
place, as Miss Sandall announced solemnly, "And let that
be a warning to you all."

PH

I was four years old, coming up to five, and the year was
1949. I was at primary school. We returned to our classes
as quiet as church mice. Sally Crowther, who sat next to
me, whispered, "I know you go home for your dinner,
but did you get back in time to see the fun?" I nodded
silently, but was not quite sure whether it really was fun;

59

certainly not for Billy - or the next child found bending a teaspoon during school dinner.

The incident of Billy Jones and the bent teaspoon was one of my early experiences of school. There were just two classes, and Miss Sandall took the older class, and was headmistress. She was described as strict. I was in the younger class, and our teacher was Miss Dellow. Everybody said how lovely she was, and she had never been known to spank any of the children. But then, Miss Sandall had caught Billy Jones bending a teaspoon, which we all decided must be a dreadful thing to do.

We were a more disciplined society in those days, and there are those who would say that that was the reason we were called Great Britain, and not just Britain. Our little village school was a State school, and our dress code was smart casual. Private schools dressed more formally in blazers and ties that were part of the school uniform. When the teacher entered the room, we stood to our feet in silence until told to sit. We learnt to read, and write with joined up letters, do sums and recite our multiplication tables. Wrong answers to simple questions, or inattention, resulted in having to stand in the corner with one's hands on one's head. And should you bend a teaspoon.... well, we had been warned.

"Let's play 'i. You're i'." And we tore around the playground, cannoning into one another as well as bystanders, and invariably ending up with grazed knees from falls. It was tag, except that nobody called it tag. It was called 'It', but no-one seemed to pronounce the 't'. And the i' was virtually spat out. *I'*! The reader is invited to try for themselves. *I'*. I made my first friends at school. My parents described Graham as the spoilt boy, Ivan was the sportsman, Neil came from a poor home, little red-haired Jenny had quite a temper, ('Redheads usually have a temper. Your grandfather almost married one, but realised in time.' I was to hear that veiled warning again and again during my childhood - and did not marry a redhead), and David was a very bright boy indeed. I wonder how other parents described me! But we were just mates who played together. Life was carefree, so long as you paid attention, learnt your tables, and did not bend teaspoons.

But this curly-haired boy paid attention, learnt his tables, steered clear of teaspoons - and loved school. Writing was fun, and reading even more so. We learnt our multiplication 'Times Tables' by rôte, chanting through the 'one times' and then the 'two times' with Miss Dellow leading loudly. There were those who found it a bore, a drudgery to be endured, but to me it was an adventure. And somehow, reading, writing, sums, and multiplication, all made sense. And playtime was looked forward to and enjoyed, whilst the sun shone down.

"What do you want to do when you grow up?" we were asked in class by Miss Dellow one morning. "We will start at the back and each in turn will say what they want to be when they leave school one day." I remember the occasion clearly, as I racked my brain for ideas on what I might do when I left school. I had not actually realised that one day I would leave school. My brain was only four or five years old. And the result of that quest for knowledge demonstrated emphatically that we were a rural, agricultural community. "So we are starting with you, Jim."

"Farmer, Miss Dellow."
"And you Michael?"
"Farmer, Miss Dellow."

"And you Graham?"
"Farmer, Miss Dellow."
"And you Rita?"
"Farmer, Miss Dellow."
 "Ivan?"
"Fireman, Miss Dellow."
"Russell?"
"Farmer, Miss Dellow."
"Beryl?"
"Nurse, Miss Dellow."
"David?"
"Farmer, Miss Dellow."

BL

And out of around thirty pupils, over twenty, including many of the girls present, replied with the words, "Farmer, Miss Dellow." And what did I say? "Farmer, Miss Dellow," because, having no idea what I wanted to do when I left school, it seemed a safe bet to identify with the majority. Many of the children lived on farms in tied accommodation, and their fathers worked as labourers or with livestock, but I did not have a clue as to what my father did all day. He 'went to work'. There may only have been two teachers at the school, but I would imagine that recounting the incident later produced a smile in the staff room. If there was a staff room, at such a small institution.

Classrooms had not changed since my parents' schooldays. Rows of wooden desks, twenty to thirty in number, each with a matching wooden chair, facing forward. Each desk had an inkwell, into which we dipped our pens. They had inter-changeable nibs, which might be fine, medium or broad, determining the writing style. At the front of the classroom was a wooden platform on which stood a larger wooden desk, with matching chair, behind which sat the teacher. Or very often stood.

In primary schools, each classroom had a large heavy blackboard on a sturdy easel, with a narrow ledge for sticks of chalk, with which to write on the board, and a duster with which to erase. Periodically, either the teacher or a pupil would walk backwards into the blackboard and there would be a tremendous crash as it fell over. Health and safety - what was that? It would be decades before those words became the bureaucratic irritation, or nightmare, as some view them today. But I cannot recall any pupil or member of staff being injured by such incidents.

Later on at secondary school, the blackboards were fixed to the walls. All text books were provided, as were the exercise books in which we wrote. Smudges, poor spelling, and crossed out words, could bring a rebuke from the teacher.

There was little or no homework at the primary school, but that changed significantly when we proceeded to secondary school, especially if it was a grammar school.

To a four-year-old boy, the classroom in the primary school seemed so large, with all those desks, and so many children. I was used to a dining room, sitting room, kitchen, and other domestic rooms. This was new and this was big.

"It's so small," referring to the primary school classroom, was a comment made repeatedly at school re-unions. Our perception of the world at four years continues in our memory, until we are confronted with a new perception, such as the same room at, say, fifty years of age. Likewise our assembly hall at the Paston School, the grammar school I later attended, where we sat shoulder to shoulder and sang hymns and psalms. "How did we all fit in?" is a rhetorical question echoing round the walls at Old Boys functions held there.

****

In 1953, our family moved to the village of Wroxham, seven miles north of Norwich in the Broadland area of Norfolk, due to my father's work. It was the year of the coronation, and at school we all made cardboard coronation coaches, and were given a commemorative mug. It was also the year of the east coast floods, and my parents would drive us to seaside villages where we would view devastated houses in which lives had been lost.

Aged eight, I was still with the little children, and now in Mrs. Shreeve's class at Wroxham County Primary School. We recited simple poems, sang simple songs, learnt to spell, and write longer words. I was the new boy in class, and wanted to impress those who had been there forever. It was playtime, and as they gathered round to assess what a boy from the back of beyond was like, I gazed at them intensely and said loudly, "Bugger!" Some gasped, and there followed a profound silence as they stared at me incredulously. Clearly they realised that I was no little pipsqueak from the middle of nowhere, but a man of words to be reckoned with. And to emphasise my relative sophistication, I looked them in the eye and repeated, "Bugger". Tom Watson pointed at me and said accusingly, "You said bugger. He said bugger. The new boy said bugger." A teacher, attracted by the silence and pointing finger, came over to see what was happening. "The new boy said 'bugger'", volunteered a freckle-faced lad, as if I had committed an unforgivable sin. "So did Tom", added another. "He said bugger *three* times." "New boy, and Tom. Come with me," said the teacher, and we traipsed off in the direction of the headmaster's study. "So, you have been swearing in the playground, have you?", said Mr. Mattocks, making it a statement rather than a question. "He said it first," said Tom. "Children who swear here get the cane," said the headmaster, reaching up to a shelf and grasping a bamboo rod. "Hold out your hands." One stroke apiece, and apart from the shock that it happened at all, largely symbolic and almost a joke. But not at age eight, and no doubt a warning to all who heard about it.

BL

And then the contrast, the unexpected, the almost unthinkable, and from a teacher. It happened a few years later at the grammar school where a new French master arrived. He was different, relaxed and jocular. Mr. Robbins (nickname Marty, after the contemporary pop singer of that name) was known to have several children, when news circulated that his wife had given birth to yet another. At the end of a lesson, he enquired, "Any questions?", whereupon the boldest of the bold asked nothing concerning cross-Channel verbs, nouns or adjectives, but, "What are you going to call your new child, sir?" Without hesitation, Sir replied, "Little bugger. Same as the others. Class dismissed."

Conkers, marbles, cigarette cards, paper aeroplanes - everything had its season in the primary school playground. A conker is the seed of the horse chestnut tree, and appeared in autumn. Suspended on string threaded through a hole in the conker, we would take turns to strike each other's conker until one shattered. After the first victory, it was a oner, and after the second a two-er, and so on. There was no neutral authentication, and those boasting a twenty-er or thirty-er were held in awe by the gullible, and suspicion by the majority. Conkers were sometimes heated in the oven, or soaked in brine overnight; everyone had their method of strengthening their weapon. Marbles was a springtime game, usually played by throwing or rolling one's marble in an attempt to hit the opponent's. Cigarette cards (thrown with the intention of landing on, and thereby attaining, ones opponent's) was another springtime activity; and then some lad would make a paper aeroplane, and within days, the air would be full of them. But in less than a week we became bored with aeroplanes, and it was back to tag, or the next craze. And the sun kept shining down.

BL

"Who's the prime minister? Who's the foreign secretary? Who's the Archbishop of Canterbury? What's the name of the Queen's husband." These, and a thousand other questions, were thrown at me by my mother. It was 1956, and she wanted me to pass the eleven-plus exam. It would determine what later career I might follow, she told me. And my income. My mother emphasised all this to me, praying I would pass and get to the grammar school (academic) and not go to the secondary modern school (technical). I took the exam and was borderline. I re-sat it and passed. A cousin of mine failed, went to the secondary modern school, and became an extremely successful architect. Two years later, my sister passed first time.

I thought that discipline had been strict at the primary schools, but it was now off the end of the scale. The Paston School in North Walsham had a military tradition, and boasted that Admiral Horatio Lord Nelson had been its finest pupil. The Norwich School, a private establishment in the nearby city, also boasted he had been *their* finest pupil. It was rumoured he had been to 'Paston' for three days and run away, before later being expelled from the Norwich School. But that was just schoolboy banter. We wore navy blue blazers, with three brass buttons. They were to be polished every day. Should one's buttons be inspected and deemed not to have been polished, one could be sent to the headmaster. Blazers were to be buttoned up, unless it was announced in morning assembly that they could be left undone. Otherwise, if not buttoned up, one could be sent to the headmaster. There was a morning assembly with hymn, psalm, reading and prayers. The hymns usually had a military ring to them - Onward Christian Soldiers, Fight the Good Fight, et al.

There was a combined cadet force (CCF), and on Friday afternoon, every boy was in uniform and marching. The cadet band played 'Colonel Bogey', and the naval cadets made strange whistling noises. Following the first year of basic training, there was an exam, after which cadets opted for army, navy, air force or band. I missed several weeks of training and the basic test due to a broken leg, and was excused thereafter. It was not an accident, and should never have happened.

There was bullying. It was one such incident that put me in hospital and kept me from school for six weeks. And yet I was not the prime target of bullies. That dubious honour would probably go to my friend Terry Howman. At school he was Howman T. C. (I have slightly changed his name). He was bullied relentlessly, and on leaving school, was admitted to a psychiatric hospital, and never came out. He was shorter than most, and slight of build. His narrow, densely freckled face had a thatch of auburn hair combed forwards. Today he might be described as cute. He spoke with a slight lisp, but he should never have lost his adulthood to a psychiatric institution. Life at home was not ideal for Terry, with his mother confined to a wheelchair, and his father working long hours on their smallholding on the outskirts of a tiny Norfolk village. His parents had coached him on answering the question, "What is your name?" He always answered, "Howman. First *how* and then *man*". Always. Totally predictably, after a while. He loved the English language, and his dream was to write a column in a national newspaper. "Like Cassandwa", Terry would lisp, alluding to the famous William Connor, who wrote a humorous and sometimes rather acid column under the pseudonym Cassandra in the *Daily Mirror* during the 1950s and 1960s. Terry tried to learn one new word a day, and would use the word as often as possible during the day. Which resulted in him asking a girl on the school bus, "Can I have an intercourse with you please?" He explained to me later, "I only wanted a conversation. I'm sure it means conversation". But older and bigger boys would heartlessly pick on Terry, snatching his school satchel and tipping out the contents, and generally pushing, pinching and insulting him.

And then his mother died. My mother drove out to see how Mr. Howman was coping, and would periodically help with the laundry. Terry's sister was mature for her age, and adopted many of the chores previously carried out by her mother. But the challenge of life at home without mother, and the incessant bullying at school, which should have been resolved by prefects and staff, resulted in Terry being admitted to a psychiatric hospital soon after leaving school, and never coming out again.

PH

I felt so sad for him, and looking back several decades on, I am appalled that he was not protected. Nobody was disciplined. But I only went to hospital with two fractures and a dislocation, and out in three days. And back to school in six weeks. Compared to Terry, I got off lightly.

Ronnie Harvey, or Harvey R. D. (again I have changed the name) was of average size in the first form, but suddenly grew taller and broader. With his swarthy complexion and black greasy hair, he looked rough and spoke rough. Many of the pupils at school would be described as middle class, and Big Ronnie felt the need to assert himself. We were standing on the paved area in front of the pavilion, waiting for it to be unlocked in order to change for football. Harvey wanted to be noticed, and for some reason, chose me as a target. "Get Snowball", he shouted. "'awk at 'im". Hawk was slang amongst the roughs for spit, and Snowball was my nickname. He made a loud guttural rasping sound, and spat in my direction. Then he again shouted, "Get 'im", and launched himself in my direction. I fled. As I careered round the side of the pavilion, I realised Harvey was catching up. I tore round the back of the building, along the far side, and emerged on the paved area at the front. My pursuer shouted, "Trip 'im" - and somebody obliged. I crashed onto the flagstones, and everybody stood laughing until someone interjected, "Look at his leg. His foot's sticking out the side." Our home overlooked the playing field, and a small group of boys carried me home, where my mother called an ambulance. Two bones were fractured, and there was a dislocation. My foot 'stuck out the side'. Six weeks away from school. Crutches for much of the time, which I was not taught to use, and which resulted in a somewhat bent spine. My parents received a letter of apology from the headmaster, but as far as I know, nobody was disciplined, and I suspect mouths were kept shut tight for fear of Big Ronnie; well, who wants a broken leg for squealing? My mother naïvely said to me, "I expect Harvey will be your friend for life after what he did to you". On my return to school six weeks later, the lout came over to me and said, "Next time, I'll break both your legs".

In another instance of bullying, one fourth-former was found to be demanding cash from first and second formers, unless they wanted to be beaten up. Protection money at an early age. Then the same boy was arrested for burglary, involving thousands of cigarettes. He was expelled.

The last I heard of him was when I read in a national daily paper that he was apprehended by police after a car chase through Brighton, in which he was firing at them through the vehicle window with a shotgun. Yes, he was a bully. During a mock battle using blanks in our weapons, whilst in the cadet force, some of the big boys told the little boys (including me) that we were to put pebbles in the barrels of our .303 rifles, and shoot the headmaster. We were threatened, but simply pretended to put pebbles in our rifle barrels. And as the school congregated in St. Nicholas church for the funeral of a previous headmaster, the same big boys demanded that the little boys spit on the coffin as it passed. Idle threats, and not without humour, when reflected on from sixty years after the events. There was an overhead pipe with a tap over a path by the bogs (toilets). Big boys would drag little boys under the tap, turn it on, and drench them. It was called 'ducking'. On one occasion, after I had been ducked, I walked through the playground soaked and dripping, to be apprehended by one of the masters, with the question, "What happened to you?". I nonchalantly answered that I had been ducked. I was naïve. But ducking was a normal part of life, wasn't it? It happened to little boys all the time, didn't it? The master was incredulous. Around a dozen 'big boys' were marched off to the headmaster, and were relieved to get away with a warning.

But most boys sent to the headmaster were not let off with a warning. He was an ex-Colonel, tall and formidable. His first name was Kenneth, and always referred to by the boys as 'Ken'. "You'll get sent to Ken," we would say to one another. There was no short bamboo stick on his shelf, and tales of his canings with a rattan rod were fearsome. Our first-year classroom looked out across the front of the boarding house towards the external door that led to the headmaster's study. Several times a week the class would freeze at the spectacle of a pleading pupil being taken by a master through the door that led to 'the imperial staircase' and up to his study. Five or ten minutes later the boy, often well into his teens, would emerge with swollen tear-filled eyes, red-faced and holding his rear quarters. The vast majority of us took note, and were extremely careful not to offend in any way. In fact, I cannot remember any one of our class being caned throughout our time there. What a deterrent. Later, in the sixth form, our library was under the head's study, and there would be a respectful silence as whacks sounding like shots from a gun were followed by cries of anguish. One of the prefects said to us, "You should see the dust come flying out of their trousers when he whacks them!" I felt that Harvey R. D. should have been whacked, and even more, those who made life intolerable for Howman T. C.

However, there was a degree of ambivalence in the attitudes of both pupils and staff with regard to corporal punishment. Pupils would speak in hushed respectful tones of recent canings, and yet would laugh together at how poor Jim was red-eyed for days following his beating. It was serious, and it was also funny?

It was Speech Day, at which the headmaster would give his annual glowing report of the school's achievements during the past year. An invited dignitary would then address the school, and proceed to present prizes and awards. Each year we were told that the esteemed gentleman was famous, though usually none of us had heard of him. One year it was Sir Thomas Armstrong. He was not the Member of Parliament of that name, executed for treason in 1684, but the headmaster's brother-in-law, and principal of the Royal College of Music. Another year it was Air Marshall, Sir Dermot Boyle, who arrived by helicopter on the school lawn. Sir Barnes Wallis was known to every pupil, as he had invented the bouncing bomb of Dambusters fame. That film was our Christmas treat almost every December. One year it was a famous Scottish headmaster, who nobody had heard of, who came from a famous Scottish school that no-one had heard of. I have forgotten his name, but can remember part of his speech. "When you boys south of the border misbehave, you are beaten with a cane. But in Scotland, we use the tawse. In case you don't know, it is a heavy, painful strap, with the business end split into two tails. People sometimes ask me whether 'tawse' is a singular or plural word. I tell them that it is singular at one end and plural at the other." There was a great explosion of laughter from headmaster and staff, but a frozen silence across the ranks of pupils. Reflecting on the man's remark, it was indeed funny. But not to the pupils of the Paston School in the late 1950s, where staff would occasionally give very stern warnings concerning the consequences of bad behaviour.

On another occasion, a former teacher was speaking on the radio. There was more than a hint of sadism when he spoke of being interviewed for a position, teaching in a boys school. He said he had been told, "The pay isn't very generous, but you do get to thrash a few boys." Both interviewer and the man himself chuckled at the thought.

There were little boys and big boys. There was no absolute definitive distinction, but the first and second formers were always little, and by the fourth form, we were big. Trouser length gave more than a hint as to which category a boy fell into; short trousers were worn by little boys and long trousers were worn by big boys. Generally. So around late second form through to early fourth form, a lad who had always worn short trousers would arrive at school one day sporting long trousers. It was not an official ceremony, but a crowd would gather around the unfortunate, jeering and shouting, "He's got long 'uns on.'" It happened to each of us, and I don't think anyone escaped the embarrassment accompanying this blend of metamorphosis and bar mitzvah. But there was always at least one second former striding round in long 'uns, and the occasional fourth former whose parents had yet to fork out for them. But times change, and cultures evolve, such that in the U.K. today, even the tiniest of boys wears long trousers, whilst someone wearing shorts is probably a Norfolk postman.

BL

There were around four hundred pupils, all boys. Around forty were boarders. There was a staff of approximately twenty-five, all male. The masters wore black gowns, and occasionally mortar boards. The only female member of staff was the school secretary. And a cleaner or two. Every master had a nickname, and most no doubt knew what they were called. And probably enjoyed it. Mr. Humphrey Grantham-Hill was *Granny*. Mr. Tyler was *Watt*, and Mr. Lamb was *Charlie* – both of historical origin and featured at some point in the curriculum. A tall swarthy man with military bearing, black centre-parted hair and flamboyant handle-bar moustache, Mr. Hawdon was held in awe by all. He was reputed to have worked with booby-traps behind the Japanese lines in World War Two. He was *Harry*. Mr. Atkinson, the Latin master, was *Voco* (pronounced Wocko). The first word he taught us in Latin was voco, translated 'I call'. The surname of Mr. Havercroft, an English master, was an anagram of hovercraft, but his nickname was *Doker*. Its origin and meaning was a mystery. And so on.

Boys were known by surname and initials; I was Lawrence B R and my friend was Woodcock J E. Burton J was a really nice guy, and Burton G was the opposite. Burton J was everybody's friend, and Burton G was everybody's nightmare. Burton G left prematurely, and no one was sorry. Spicer J hoped to be a vet one day, Spellman D aspired to join the prison service, and his close mate Mellor B wanted to be a bigtime crook. All ambitions were realised, and I sometimes wonder whether Spellman and Mellor met up again in later years. However, most were known by nicknames, whose origins were long forgotten. Where did *Gully* come from, and what was the origin of *Shadley*? *Four Eyes* was very sensitive about wearing spectacles and cried when the name was used. Eventually his class was told that anyone heard using the name would be punished. John Spicer was *Spike*, and Dave Bird had no objection to being called *Dickie*. *Titch* was short, *Stalky* was tall and thin, and Beaky had a big nose. *Snowball*? That was me, from day one at grammar school, because of my head of very fair, curly hair. Most nicknames were borne with good humour, but I must confess to feeling a mixture of pity and revulsion every time my eyes fell on the rather grubby young toad known as *Bog Rat*. In the fourth form, aged around fifteen, we started asking one another what the Christian name initials stood for, and would inexplicably crease up laughing at the revelation of 'John' or 'Peter' or 'Joseph' or indeed, 'Barrie'.

"Lawrence, your shoe lace is undone," said Lincoln J. I forget his second initial. He was gazing at my shoe, and looking concerned. I glanced down, preparing to kneel and retie the bow. "Which one?" I asked, a little perplexed and quite aware by now that both laces were still tied.

"April Fool," he shouted in my face, and tore off across the playground. It was spring 1957.

Well, two could play at that game, and I scanned the area, selected my victim, and approached Buck D. I kept my eyes focussed on his feet, and trying to sound genuinely concerned for his welfare, observed, "Buck, your shoe lace is undone."

"Idiot, Lawrence! You're the fifth this morning. Do try and be a little more creative." Buck D was much brighter than me. He had a way with words. We had been at Wroxham County Primary School together, and he had passed the eleven-plus examination first time. Buck D was an A-streamer at grammar school, and I was a B-streamer. It showed. It usually does.

I was unsuspecting. Mother had come into my bedroom that morning quite early, as she always did. She felt it was necessary to ensure that I was awake and ready for school. She had thrown open the curtains, and gasped, "It's been snowing all night. Everywhere is white." I loved snow and leapt out of bed like a super-animated kangaroo, bounded to the window, and... "Snow? I can't see any."

"April Fool!"

She did this every year, and without fail, I leapt out of bed, bounced to the window...

And so back to school. Schools take pride in former pupils who have excelled in their field, or perhaps become famous. So many of our prime ministers are the boast of just one school, and so many went to just one other school. None went to the Paston School. But we had one former pupil who outshone all others. Horatio, Lord Nelson. Nelson was born in Norfolk, and had family connections to our first *de facto* prime minister,

Robert Walpole. He is undoubtedly our most famous old boy.

There were four houses at the school, and each was named after a former pupil of whom the school was proud. Nelson, Tenison, Warton and Hoste. Nelson - we had all heard of Nelson, and the Battle of Trafalgar, and some knew something about Lady Hamilton. And there was Hardy, of whom a kiss was requested. But the other famed three? Tenison - yes, many of us thought we had heard of him too. "*Not* that one", we were told. "Our Tenison has an 'i'. He was Archbishop of Canterbury from 1694 to 1715, and crowned two monarchs". Warton was poet laureate in 1785. Hoste? - Captain Sir William Hoste was a contemporary of Nelson, and probably of equal valour. Nelson was a pupil for just two years from 1769 to 1771; two centuries later, another pupil arrived, who would also achieve fame. But Stephen Fry departed in a lot less than two years. There is no school house named Fry.

Whichever house pupils were in (I was in Nelson), one could not get away from 'our immortal hero'. There was a Nelson Room, also used as the music room, and packed with Nelson memorabilia. This included a brick, set in a glass case, and with the initials *HN* scratched into it. Were they really the work of the, perhaps, 12-year-old himself? Did anyone see him do it? Was he whacked for it? But it is certainly an ancient brick, and perhaps the initials are as old as the brick. Nevertheless, when one visited the bogs (latrines to accommodate around twenty boys), one could find dozens of bricks with the initials *HN* scratched into them. More schoolboy humour!

Tenison, Warton and Hoste get a mere mention in the school song, but Nelson has the best part of a verse. In fact, seven of the eleven lines of a verse. (The song originally had six verses of eleven lines. Thankfully, by the time I attended, it had been reduced to three verses). It is still sung at the Old Boys dinner, held on the Saturday nearest to Trafalgar Day (21st October) each year.

I have never been an academic, and had to study long hours in order to retain what I was taught. I never excelled on the sports field, but represented the school once in the tennis team. Long distance running was my forté, but even then, I was usually placed around fourth. I was mediocre at most subjects, and just passed each of my GCE Ordinary level examinations. Every other student gained distinctions and merits, but each failed in at least one subject, and unbelievably, I was deemed to have come first in the fifth year. In fact, I felt that a mistake had been made, and went to the school secretary to inform her. I had never won a prize before in my days at grammar school. She explained the system, and I was indeed first in the fifth year. I had seven passes; just about everybody else had distinctions and merits, but had also failed in at least one subject, and so the pupil in second place had six passes. As a result, on Prize Day I marched across the stage and shook hands with the famous and afore-mentioned Sir Barnes Wallis, inventor of the Dambuster's bouncing bomb, and Wellington bomber, and received my award with pride.

Schooldays, I loved them. They were days of learning, growing, adventure, and of making a few friendships that would last for decades. There was a definite downside, with the background of bullying and serious discipline, but my overall memories are of a positive nature. Schooldays lived under a big blue Norfolk sky.

Chapter Five

My Norfolk Birds!

Chased by 'the hag', ravished in a tunnel, snogging behind a gooseberry bush, and Mrs. Starling's beak.

It was late, and it was dark, as she grasped my hand ever more tightly and pulled me sharply to the right, with the words, "This way." Of course, I remembered, there was a pedestrian tunnel here. It was unlit, and I was unsuspecting, as I was suddenly clutched, engulfed, and almost devoured by this teenaged siren-supreme.

****

It was 1960, and at fifteen, coming up to sixteen, newly acquired hormones were tumbling through my veins, and I was trying to discover my real identity. Like my friends, who were equally driven and no less naïve.

With those unfamiliar hormones now bombing through my cardiovascular system, 'birds' were becoming of ever-increasing interest. A new coffee bar in the high street, with floor to ceiling plate glass windows facing the street, was known locally as the goldfish bowl. My friends and I would gather there, sitting like morons, peering out, while passers-by gawped back. Sipping coffee. Staring. Grinning at one another and saying, "We're bird watching!" We would leer out of those glass walls as the birds strutted by. It was a game, but we never realised. The birds slowed down, dithered, and flashed the hint of a smile and an inordinate portion of thigh, before continuing past. I felt self-conscious. Surely everybody was staring at me, and was interested in me. But they were only interested in themselves, and were as self-conscious as I was. We were teenagers.

BL

Forgive me, for I was an innocent fifteen-year-old. The word 'bird' to describe a teenage girl is unacceptable today; it is sexually dismissive. But not to teenaged boys living in rural Norfolk in the 1960s. So what was its origin? Around the year 1300, the word *burde* appeared in the English language. A burde was a young maiden, and the term cropped up periodically during the succeeding centuries. However, the word *bird* to mean young woman was not used until 1915, and is possibly unrelated to burde. And then this use of the word bird exploded in the 1950s and 1960s, and simultaneously, the word *chick* in the United States. There was no equivalent word for young men, because society was, generally, not sexually dismissive towards men. Maybe, when I was a few years older, I would be called a bloke. Now back to the boy Barrie and his hormones.

My awareness of *la différence* had been aroused some years earlier. It was at primary school, aged nine or ten, that I had first fallen in love. Sandra Golder. She sat in front of me in class, and I would gaze at her blonde hair, and when she turned round, her big blue eyes would make me catch my breath. I made the mistake of confiding in a friend, who then confided in Sandra. The rat. How embarrassing. The next day a little crumpled note lay on my desktop. It read, 'Kiss my hand. Sandra'.

And during the first lesson of the day, Sandra sat very awkwardly at her desk, and somehow twisted her arm through the back of her chair, looking almost deformed in the process. I was too shy to kiss it, but touched it lightly with two fingers, simulating a kiss. She thought I had consummated the relationship, and, as my heart pounded, her neck turned deep scarlet. At the end of lessons, she was off like a hare, out of the door and home before I could so much as wink at her. We exchanged love letters, of around three sentences each, on more pieces of crumpled paper. We exchanged rings, made of plastic, which probably originated in Christmas crackers, and changed hands in the playground for a few old pennies a time.

BL

She confided in me that her surname was not really Golder at all, but Forbes, and nobody else knew. Where might this *affaire de coeur* have ended, had her family not suddenly moved to another part of the country? Goodbye Sandra.

Hello Barbara. Also known as 'the hag'. Plop! A pink envelope with a border of coloured hearts landed on our doormat, hidden amongst a plethora of brown commercial mail. Plop! It was breakfast time, and Father dropped it onto my placemat. "For you," he said with a grin.

I stared at the envelope. Aged eleven, I never received post. Except on birthdays. Post was for grown-ups. And this was, well... pretty. For me? Surely there was a mistake, because I received neither post nor pretty things. All eyes were on me, and overcome with curiosity, I inserted my breakfast knife into the envelope and having slit it open, withdrew the most amazing card.

A huge heart. Pink. Purple. Glitter. 'Sweetheart'. 'Love'. 'Darling'. 'Forever'. And no signature, but an enigmatic question mark. I was totally confused. Nonplussed. Baffled and befuddled. I stared at the card. And then stared some more.

"Mummy, is this from you?" I asked, totally bewildered. "What is it? I know you love me."
"Nothing to do with me," said mother. And as I looked at my father, he grinned and shook his head. "Nothing to do with me either." And I was sure it was not from my sister.
"Maybe it's one of those Valentine cards I've read about in the newspaper," said mother. "I think it's some American craze. Most crazes come from America." And then, with lowered voice and the hint of a smile, "Do you have a secret girlfriend?"
I thought of Sandra, and the feigned kiss and scruffy little love notes, and felt myself going scarlet with embarrassment.
"No girlfriends," I stammered.
"Well, it certainly looks as though you have a secret admirer, young man. You'd better watch out for her, because that's an expensive card she's sent you."

I was just eleven years old. I had never heard of Valentine's Day. Nor had my parents, except mother had seen something recently in the *Daily Mail*. But Barbara had. Barbara lived at the top of the road, and was a year younger than me. She was one of a small group of girls who would stand around the edge of the park where I and some of my friends would spend endless hours playing football. They were tall and short and plump and thin. And giggly. I avoided them.

"The hag has got a crush on you," said Roger the Rough. He was my best mate. He was a little younger than me, and in Barbara's class at school.
"Barbara," he replied knowingly. "Barbara Haggitty. The hag!"

She was skinny, with straggly, mousy hair, and big teeth. I noticed teeth. And giggly. She wore a pale red gingham dress, and sloppy blue cardigan. And she just would not take her eyes off me. As I and my footballing friends left the park, the girls would drift to the gateway and chatter and giggle as we passed. And the hag would stare hard at me.

It was some days later. "Something for you," said mother, placing a small pink envelope beside my plate at supper time. "It came through the letter box late afternoon. There's no stamp on it. Just the words 'For Barrie', and it's lumpy. I should open it carefully."
"Go on. Open it," said my sister, grinning in a teasing manner.
"Expect it's that secret admirer again," said my father.

Embarrassment. I ignored the envelope, and tucked into my beef stew. No-one else was eating, and every eye was riveted on the pink envelope.
"Go on. Open it," said my sister, "Or I'll open it for you!"
I snatched it from the table, and slowly slit the top open. Inside were small objects.
I gently tipped them out onto the table cloth.
"Love hearts. You've got love hearts. She's after you, that admirer girl. She must be in love with you. Hey,

what do they say?" said my sister, and suddenly, they were snatched from me, and I had to endure the catalogue of,

BL

"*Let's Kiss,*" followed by shrieks of laughter. "*Be Mine* - well she's making her intentions clear." "Certainly is," from my father. "*My Love*", followed by giggling, and "Are you sure you don't have a secret lover?" from my father. "*Dreaming Of You* - I wonder what her dreams are like? Here's the last, *I'll Get You!*" I snatched them back, and found that the final '*I'll Get You*' was not there at all. My sister had made it up. My face and neck were burning with embarrassment, and amidst remarks concerning diamond rings and wedding bells and the patter of tiny feet, I struggled through my stew, potatoes and asparagus, and hastily left to go and play football. (A word of explanation, in case you have not been down this road in life. Love hearts were, maybe continue to be, hard, coloured tablet shaped sweets in a variety of flavours, each with a love message).

In the park at the top of the road, my mates were chatting together. But there was bad news amongst them, in the form of a pale red gingham dress, and straggly hair in pigtails. Also, a couple of her friends, all whispering and sniggering.

"Wotcher Barrie. Guess what?" said Shadley. (Shadley? Michael Brown, but Shadley to us. It was his nickname and neither he nor anyone else had a clue as to its origin. "I've been called Shadley for years and years. All my life really," the ten-year-old had told me when he first joined our group in the park). "Barbara wants to play football

with us. We've told her she can't, cos it's a boys' game."
And everybody was grinning.

JW

BL

"Then let's play a game that we *can* all play," said
Barbara. She looked at me and smiled broadly. My, those
front teeth were huge. "I want to play kiss chase," she
almost laughed out.
"Great idea," said Roger the Rough. The rat. And they
were all grinning at me. "Yeah. And you can go first
Barbara," said Shadley. Rats indeed - it was a conspiracy.
"Count to ten, and see who you can catch," shouted a
scruffy young freckle-faced urchin. And as about ten
pairs of eyes leered at me, Barbara started counting, and
quite quickly too. "One, two, three, four...." Suddenly
everybody was running. And no-one faster than me. Like
a hare, I reached the fencing surrounding the park, and
paused to look over my shoulder. Yikes, the gingham
clad hag was coming my way - and fast. I sped along by
the fence, and she moved to cut me off, crossing the park
diagonally. I stopped suddenly, turned around, and sped
towards the gate where we had come in. But shock horror
- Roger and Shadley had closed the gate and were
standing blocking the way, and laughing hysterically.
Again I stopped. And before I could make a further dash,
they had jumped forward and grabbed me.
"Got 'im," Roger shouted. "He's all yours Barbara." And
then to me, "It's alright mate. She'll just give you a quick
snog, and then you get to chase who *you* fancy." And
then another shout, "We'll hold him for you." Panic. The
hag was coming my way fast, closing in on me, and with

those large front teeth pointing very much in my direction. I was sweating!

As Roger and Shadley shook with laughter, their grip loosened. I pushed them away with both arms and again fled, this time towards the woods bordering the far side of the park, and towards which I should have headed earlier. And then I was amongst the trees, out of the park and running like an Olympic sprinter along paths which led ultimately to the fence, behind which lay our back garden. Panels swung open, and I squeezed through into safety.

Why did it have to be the hag? Why had Sandra's family moved away? If Sandra had chased me, I would have run slowly. And probably into the woods! And those teeth. Did they have Spear and Jackson, or Armitage Shanks engraved on the back, I mused. More schoolboy humour.

And then, out of the blue, I escaped from this increasingly threatening situation.
"The bank has moved Daddy to North Walsham, and we are leaving Wroxham very soon. I'm afraid you'll have to say Goodbye to your friends."

Goodbye Barbara - hag, with big front teeth. And Roger the Rough, and Shadley. Rats - but all sins quickly forgiven and mates at heart.

Hello Ann. What a bird! We had moved to North Walsham, and she lived across the other side of town, which in Norfolk, meant fifteen minutes' walk away. I was aged thirteen now, and at the boys grammar school. She was at the girls high school, and she would send messages via my younger sister. To glance at Ann made my head swim, my heart pound and my legs tremble. To be called 'Dreamland' by such a stunner took my breath away. She wanted us to have an evening together on Felmingham heath, but it never happened. Why was I so shy, when this amazing siren of a creature was making all the overtures? My hormones rattled round at breakneck speed as I tried to pluck up the courage, when........ Ann moved to New Zealand. Goodbye Ann.

Hello Carol. If Ann had been a siren making overtures, Carol went straight for the jugular. No messing. Minimal small talk. Life was too short, even at the age of fifteen. Friday evening was the highlight of the week, when lads and lasses congregated in the church hall, where we listened to music from a record player spinning vinyl on a turntable, played table tennis badly, and eyed up members of the opposite sex. I would lounge around with my mates, Beefy and Sludge. Beefy was skinny, and his real name was Keith. Sludge was fat, and his real name is forgotten. Many years later Beefy became headmaster of the First School where my young daughters started their education. I almost fell off my chair with shock. Beefy! (And as previously mentioned, I was Snowball. My hair was very fair, and on my first day at grammar school in September 1956, one of the big boys had pointed, laughed, and said how my head resembled a snowball. And from that moment on I was *Snowball*). But back to 1959, and the youth club in Vicarage Street, where the boys grouped together on one side of the room, and the girls on the other. Until the evening when Carol arrived. This was coincident with a change at the bank where my father worked as a cashier. The previous, older manager had been promoted further up the career ladder and moved to a larger branch, and a man slightly younger than my father was now big chief. He wanted to follow his predecessor up the career ladder, and ran a tight ship. My father groaned about 'these young whippersnappers' feeling they knew it all, and seeking future glory by climbing over the backs of those who really did all the work. The new man was married, with a daughter.

A redhead strode in through the door to the hall. Heads turned, and she smiled, nodded, and mouthed 'Hello' to the girls congregating at the far end of the room. Maybe she had met them before. A trim figure, twinkling eyes, a broad smile, the legs of a super model, and all at fifteen, going on twenty-five. Wow - what a bird! Who was this girl? Where had she come from? We were soon to find out.

BL

Ignoring the cluster of girls, save for the cursory smile as she entered, she made a beeline for the boys. "Hi chaps. How you doing?" She was introducing herself to the group of four or five a few paces from us, and encountering the standard greeting of that time, "Wotcher", pronounced 'Watch-uh', which was used by nearly all of my friends and acquaintances. Whether one was opening conversation with the dustman (I'm sure they are called something different these days) or the dentist, or seeing one of one's mates on the other side of the street, we uttered or shouted, 'Wotcher'. This was '60s rural Norfolk, and we were in some ways bumpkins and peasants, though I understand that the term 'Wotcher' had very wide use. But not the elegant and extremely confident young lady who had just burst in upon us, "I'm Carol," she volunteered, "And this is my first week in North Walsham. It's a bit different from the big city, but Daddy has been sent here by the bank, and I want to get to know you all". I was mesmerised, as she chatted up the lads in the group to my left. But she seemed quickly bored, and was suddenly engaging our little group of three. "I'm Carol. And who are you?" she gushed, with the broadest smile, and eyes that sparkled.

"I'm Sludge, and that's Beefy. He's my main mate," said the portly fourteen-year-old. "And that's Snowball, who's a year older than me and my mate. He wants to be a dentist. But he's OK". Sludge was always the charmer, and seemed to ask all the right questions and press all the right buttons. And although Beefy was the handsome one, I thought that Sludge was in the process of making a conquest, while shy little me just sat and observed. Until... "Snowball. Uncross your legs. I want to sit on you," left me in a state of near shock. Carol parked herself on my lap, placed an arm round my neck, and continued to make conversation with Sludge, mainly, and Beefy occasionally. I seemed to be an object to be sat on, and continued silently observing. Until... "It's time to go home. Snowball, I don't really like the dark, and I want you to walk me home. I live over the bank in the market place."

As she went to collect her coat, Beefy muttered 'Good luck' and Sludge just turned and walked away. "This way," said the amazing redhead, taking me by the hand, and leading me out of the hall and into the lamp-lit street, where we turned right, walking up the cobbled incline that led to the market place. "Not that way," said Carol, pulling me to the left. "Through the churchyard. It's a much better way home for me". I was surprised, though the market place ran parallel to the churchyard, separated by a row of shops. We walked slowly, hand in hand, past weathered stones that spoke of different lives from a different age. How long had she been in town? Did she think she would like rural Norfolk? No doubt she was going to the high school my sister attended? And then, suddenly, she grasped my hand ever more tightly and pulled me sharply to the right, with the words, "This way". Of course, I remembered, there was a pedestrian tunnel here, between and under shops, leading from the market place to the churchyard, or vice versa. The tunnel was unlit, and I was unsuspecting, as I was suddenly clutched, engulfed, and almost devoured by this fifteen-year-old siren-supreme. Her lips were hard against mine, and her tongue fought its way past my incisors, canines, premolars and molars (I knew my teeth – I was going to be a dentist!) until she was virtually massaging my tonsils. Her hands were slowly, firmly, exploring my body, and then she was taking my hands to help me explore hers. It was all quite innocent really – but not for a fifteen-year old Norfolk lad. After no more than five minutes I felt physically, mentally and emotionally exhausted. My hormones might have been rattling round every part of my body, but they were no match for Carol. We emerged from the tunnel into the moonlit market place, and walked slowly to her front door, enjoyed a long lingering kiss. We both confessed that we could not wait for another dose of youth club the following Friday.

Carol filled my thoughts, imagination, and dreams morning, afternoon, evening and night. Friday night needed a little planning, perhaps, with a shorter time at the club socialising with the other guys, and then an apologetic farewell as Carol and I left rather prematurely, for the churchyard, the tunnel, and..... but there must be other places. I shaved, washed my hair, added just the right amount of my father's *Brylcreem*, and more than a touch of *Old Spice* aftershave. I told my parents not to wait up for me, though they always did.

After walking briskly to the Youth Club, I entered, looked round to see if she had arrived before me - and could not believe my eyes. She was already there, sitting on Sludge's knee, and all over the boy. And he was only fourteen, a full year younger than me. "Sorry Snowball," said Mr. Charm. "It's my turn tonight, mate. Sort of musical chairs, ain't it darlin'! And we'd really appreciate a little privacy, cos we've a lot to talk about together, haven't we darlin'." And he pulled her closer as she ran her hands through his hair, glancing briefly in my direction, and mouthing 'Sorry'. Goodbye Carol.

Birds. I got to know them a little, and off they flew. There were others. Hello Shirley. Shirley had long blond hair and a Norfolk accent heavier than the average local ploughman. She lived in the village of Sloley, but came on to me quite quickly. I really had not noticed her, but she sent me little notes that rapidly drew my attention. Well, you do notice when letters arrive telling you that someone is in love with you. But I was not overly interested, and was now studying all hours. I had to, as I am not an academic, and needed to pass my Advanced Level GCEs in order to be accepted by dental school. I returned from trapping coypus for dissection in the biology laboratory one evening (coypus? - we come to them in chapter seven) to be greeted by my father, grinning and telling me that 'Shirley Temple' had been hammering on the door because she *wanted* me. But I needed to pass those exams. And I never really fancied her. Goodbye Shirley.

Hello Sarah. Finally, during the summer before I left for the metropolis of London, and teeth, there was Sarah.

She was to be the first of a few Sarahs, though I never married a Sarah. And then, jumping several years into the future when my wife Sheila announced that she was pregnant with our first child, I asked what she would like to call it if it was a girl. "Sarah". She came straight out with it. So I said little about Sarah who I met on the Norfolk fruit and chicken farm, or the Sarah I met hiking in the Lake District on Easter holiday during my first year at dental school. And our first daughter was indeed Sarah. What a beautiful name, and what a beautiful person and eldest daughter I have been blessed with. Whereas Sarah on the farm was relatively plain. She was a medical student from somewhere in the north of the country, using her summer to earn money. So was I, and picking broad beans on adjacent rows, and later black currants from neighbouring bushes, we struck up a friendship. The occasional smile, wink, and quick snog behind a gooseberry bush. Towards the end of summer there was a dance with a '60s beat group, organised by the farm for all those who worked there. Sarah was dolled up, but still rather plain. And when the more glamorous Cindy came over and brazenly asked me to dance, I took little persuading, and caddishly spent the evening with her. We smooched our way round the floor, and there was the occasional snog outside the back door next to the toilets. And then the summer was over. Sarah went back to the north and to medical school, and Cindy to.... but I never found out, and was not interested. I set off for the London Hospital in Whitechapel to study my chosen profession. Goodbye Sarah. Goodbye Cindy. And Goodbye to Norfolk birds for around ten years.

****

But during my teenage years in Norfolk, I encountered three types of birds. Those I have already described were in a league of their own, and of all-consuming interest. However, there was also the feathered variety. Studying biology for my 'Ordinary' level and 'Advanced' level GCE examinations, which I needed if I wanted to progress to University to study dentistry, included birds. Even though they did not have teeth. We learnt the basics concerning their anatomy, and living in the country, had a variety of species on our doorstep. There were huge flocks of starlings in those days, swirling, twisting and turning through the air in their thousands in the most amazing patterns, known as murmurations. I was a nasty young chap at times, hiding in our garden shed, clutching my air rifle, having cleared snow from the lawn and throwing down pieces of bread taken from the kitchen. Starlings would descend in such numbers that the grass, and bread, would be totally obscured. And then - but frankly, you would not really want to know, and nor would I really want to tell you.

I am no ornithologist, and during my childhood and teenage years, had a very limited interest in birds. And yet, in Norfolk, they cannot be ignored. It was during our Wroxham years in the mid-1950s, between the ages of eight and thirteen, that I became aware of different varieties of our feathered friends. Blue tits would swing on lumps of fat that my mother suspended from a tree that stood behind our rear lawn; until a great spotted woodpecker descended, and smaller birds scattered in all directions. My father would mutter about the wood pigeons swooping down from the trees behind our home, and devouring his cabbages, broccoli, cauliflowers and sprouts. Later on, in my mid-teens, crossing meadows whilst mousing and ratting, there were times when I came close to inadvertently treading on a pheasant, which would dramatically take off, almost vertically, with a loud coarse klaxon-type alarm call. I would leap back, almost as alarmed as the bird itself.

BL

Today, I have a greater appreciation and just a little more knowledge concerning these beautiful creatures. The reserve at Cley, in north Norfolk, with its visitor centre, is truly amazing, where one can enjoy a panoramic view across the marshes. Avocets, godwits, various geese, marsh harriers, and so many more - even I have learnt to recognise and almost enthuse over the wide variety of birds always present there. Strumpshaw Fen is a little to the east of Norwich, and is one of the few places where I have observed a bittern (an endangered species, a type of heron). Swallowtail butterflies are another endangered species commonly seen there during summer months.

We are indeed blessed in Norfolk to enjoy a large number of nature reserves and such a rich variety of wildlife. However, it is outside the scope of this little book to explore the subject at any length.

****

But there was a third variety of Norfolk birds. Dreary, boring, and as stuffy as they could get, and yet bringing a smile to my face from time to time, as they waddled and shuffled and fluttered around our family in those days. I first encountered them in the church that my mother decided we would attend as a family. It was our first Saturday in our new home in North Walsham when my mother announced that we would all be going to church the next morning. What? We had never been to church on Sundays, except when staying with Nana and

Grandpa. "Why church?" we asked. "Because we are Congregationalists", was the reply. "What are we? Congregagay whats?" I ventured. Mother explained that we were Congregationalists, because her father was, and there had not been a Congregational church anywhere near where we had lived in the past. So we had not been to church. Now there was, and we would.

"I'm Church of England, and I'm going to do the garden tomorrow," said my father.

Mother told him he could go to the Church of England or come with us. She often 'told him'.

"I'm an atheist. There is no God," I objected.

Mother just told me I was going to church, and that was in the days when children, generally, did what their parents told them. Today, it seems to me that parents, generally, do what their children tell them.

My sister said nothing. Sensible girl.

So we all went to church each Sunday, where the next person in age above me was often my mother. The more I listened to the preaching, the more I felt confirmed in my atheism. And if I had not gone to London.... but that's another story.

Birds. The church was full of them. In fact, the church secretary was called Mr. Bird, which meant we also had Mrs. Bird and their son, Brian Bird. Mr. and Mrs. Dove usually sat in the back pew, and Mrs. Crow used to flutter around the halfway mark. Sometimes there would be Finches, and various other birds would come and go. There are probably as many bird names amongst the population of other parts of the UK too, but I was a Norfolk boy, and it amused me. These were Norfolk birds.

"It's not a church, mother. It's a flipping aviary," I announced, and mother seemed to think that merited a smile. Otherwise, my comments on church were not welcomed, though I was expected to go as long as I was part of the family and living at home. What was the problem? Bald heads, grey hair, hearing aids and jumble sales - I write of these in another chapter. And years later, when I met evangelical Christians in London and was 'born again', announcing to my parents that I had become a Christian and now realised that the Bible *was* true, there was another groan and words of indignation. But that too is another story.

I returned to Norfolk at the end of 1973, having qualified as a dental surgeon in 1968, and after working as an associate at a practice in Dorset for five years. Now I had my own practice, and very soon, the appointment book was full. There were more Birds, Doves, Crows and Finches, but also Hawkes, Kytes, Wrens, Drakes, Woodcocks, Partridges, Goslings, Ravens, Nightingales, Jays and Buntings.

There was also Mrs. Starling, who taught my eldest daughter, Sarah, to play the violin. One day I took Sarah to one side, and explained that I had some confidential information that she might find interesting.
"Your violin teacher, Mrs. Starling, is going to marry, and will then be called Mrs. Grey. So Sarah, I won't be able to examine and treat her *beak* anymore!"
Sarah thought about this, and gave a little giggle. Mrs. Starling's beak. I told her this was confidential. Sarah was twelve, and she wanted to share the joke. But who with? Her form mistress at school was warm and friendly, and we sometimes came across her socially. So Sarah waited until the end of class, and confided in her.

"Daddy says he treats my violin teacher's *beak*, because she's called Mrs. Starling, but when she marries, she will be Mrs. Grey and won't have a beak anymore." Sarah sniggered and put her hand over her mouth. But the teacher was not amused.

"Well Sarah," she said. "I'm just glad your father is not *my* dentist."

The teacher's name was Mrs. Parrott.

Norfolk birds - they seem to be everywhere. It was only the other day I was speaking to the folks who live over the road from us, Peter and Teresa Sparrow...

Norfolk birds - exquisite!

BL

Chapter Six

Our Norfolk Holidays

Mr. Tennyson's nose, sand castles, Grandpa gets lost, and a French souvenir.

'The hardware shop in the high street is having a bath sale. They're half-price, but you have to put your own bottom in it'.

It was the early to mid 1950s, I was aged around ten and we had gone to watch the summer show, *Salad Days*, at the packed town theatre in Gorleston-on-Sea. I laughed because everybody else laughed, but I did not understand it. The joke was reckoned to be a little bit naughty. And theatre did not get much naughtier than that at family shows in the 1950s.

****

My maternal grandparents were privileged, in that having a successful business, *and* a motor car, they had enjoyed beach holidays during the summers of the 1920s and later. Devon was their favourite destination, but it would take all day to travel there from East Anglia, with no motorways or by-passes in those days. Beach holidays were an 'English invention' of the mid 18th century, when bathing in sea water was promoted as therapeutic in combating a range of health issues.

Following the *1938 Holiday Pay Act*, holidays became affordable to a large proportion of the population, and the 1950s and 1960s were the heyday of the great British seaside holiday. Generally, people travelled to their nearest resort, with Blackpool and Morecambe becoming popular with people living in the West Midlands, and Filey and Scarborough with those from Bradford and Leeds. Most travelled by rail, but my father had a car, and in view of its unreliability, chose the nearest resort to us - Gorleston-on-Sea.

Our very first holiday was to be at the seaside, and I was around five years old, and my sister two years younger. I could sense the excitement, but in no way comprehend what it was about. My parents talked about it much, and clearly preparation was being made for a change to our family routine. And then, the day before we were due to travel, I went spotty from head to toe. The doctor was called, and confirmed chicken pox. So our first ever holiday did not happen. I can only imagine the overwhelming disappointment that my parents must have experienced.

But the following year, Gorleston was booked again, and our Austin 7 successfully transported us to a guest house where we were to thoroughly enjoy our first 'week by the sea'.

"Mr. Tennyson really has got a huge nose," said my father, in lowered tones. We were having dinner in the guest house, just a few streets back from the cliff top. My parents had made brief conversation with the family, also with two children, on the adjacent table. Their name was Tennyson, and it was a fact that the man had a big nose, though I would probably not have noticed if my father had not drawn attention to it. I turned to stare at Mr. Tennyson's nose.

"Barrie. Don't stare at people", my mother whispered. And, "Dick, don't talk about Mr. Tennyson like that. You know how Barrie will react".

JW

My father finished what he was eating before quietly replying, "But it is *enormous*. If he lays on his back in the sea, and the wind catches it, he'll be in France before he knows it!" Wow, what a nose. I swung round in my seat and stared hard, and before mother could say anything, Mr. Tennyson was staring back. Even with my eyes fixed on that huge hooter, I could not miss the fact that, on either side of it, an eye was fixed on me. I blushed a little, and turned back to the table.

"I'm sorry, Mr. Tennyson. This is the first time Barrie has been on holiday, and he has never seen so many people dining in one room before". Mother too was blushing, as she whispered to me, "Don't you dare stare at Mr. Tennyson again". And to my father, "Don't provoke him like that Dick". My father whispered back, "It's just the size of his nose. *Unbelievable*". And as I was about to swing round for just one last look, a hand under the table held my knee fast, and my mother was now staring at me rather like I had been staring at Mr. Tennyson.

The holiday was unforgettable. There was a model yacht pond, and my parents bought me a small sailing boat. Sometimes it would sail across beautifully, and sometimes it would arc round and return to me. Or the wind would drop, and I would fidget impatiently, waiting for it to set sail again. There were a few older boys with much larger yachts, and those of us with tiny ones would look on with envy. There was also the occasional powerful model motor boat, which would accidentally, well, sort of 'accidentally', we suspected, ram one or two of those smarter yachts.

"I say, young man", an aggrieved father would say with restraint, "Do be careful with that thing. You could damage my Jeremy's cutter".

The amusement arcades had rows of slot machines that took pennies. The old-fashioned penny, of course, long before the new pence were introduced in 1971. Father would give me, perhaps twelve pennies. Ever hopeful, I would soon lose the lot. But father would fork out another handful the next day.

The beach was sandy, and during that first seaside holiday, my parents bought my sister and me buckets and spades, and showed us how to build sand castles. We soon learnt that the sand needed to be moist. We noticed that other sand castles were adorned with an array of little paper flags on balsa wood flagpoles, and father left us for five minutes and returned with a packet. We built a castle near the sea edge, and watched it eventually submerge under the relentless incoming tide. We paddled, but had to hold a parent's hand, unless they were very close.

BL

We were allowed one ice cream a day, and were occasionally surprised with the treat of a second one. We hovered by a *Punch and Judy* show, but my parents were unwilling to pay for seats, and we wandered on.

There was a wooden jetty going a long way out into the sea. That was my perception, aged around six or seven. Every evening, father would take me down the cliff path and along to the jetty. We would walk to the end, and gaze out to sea.

"So Barrie; which do you think will come in first tonight?" would be the question.

"*Golden Galleon*", I might reply, to which my father would probably tender, "Well, I'll say the *Eastern Princess*". And we would stand there, proudly bonding, as we waited for the first hazy puff of smoke to appear on the horizon. My father would hold back, and allow me to be the one to shout, "I can see them". The three pleasure steamers would be returning from their trip to the Scroby Sands and back, and the order was usually different each evening. And perhaps that evening it would be the *Norwich Belle* leading the way, and we would walk back to the guest house hand in hand, with me noting that tomorrow evening it would have to be the *Eastern Princess* that came in first. Or the *Golden Galleon*.

That holiday was, for me, an amazing, unforgettable experience of paradise under a cobalt sky. Fun time with my parents and sister, ice creams, beach, and so much more.

BL

Around seventy years on, I can still sense the excitement of guessing the order of the returning pleasure steamers, of making those sand castles, and paddling in swirling, tickling shallow water. And of course, Mr. Tennyson's nose.

Gorleston-on-Sea ('Gorleston' to most local people) was our holiday destination for several years. My Aunt Marie had returned from teaching children of the military stationed in Germany and was now at a school in Gorleston. We would visit her (and the model yacht pond) from time to time. She was only an hour's drive away by Austin 7 (perhaps thirty minutes today), and she thought we would love to go to the summer show where the comedian made a joke about baths and bottoms.

My paternal grandparents from Peterborough joined us on a second Gorleston holiday, and made the time especially memorable by buying me a large model yacht. The varnished deck gleamed, and the whole object was so very light. Grandpa would gaze on proudly as young Barrie would adjust the sails, launch the craft, and often have to sprint round to the far side due to the speed of the vessel. I was blessed with such lovely grandparents, and remember each of them so fondly. They made time for me. They listened to me. They spoilt me, as grandparents should!

All our early holidays were beach holidays, and Great Yarmouth was my parents' favourite destination. Yarmouth (most local people omit the Great) lies immediately to the north of Gorleston, across the river Yare. Both were ports, and heavily involved with the herring fishing industry until the mid 1950s. Yarmouth became a major holiday resort, known to some as the Blackpool of the East.

Great Yarmouth owes its existence to the simple herring, a coastal fish, silvery in colour, usually a little under 30cm in length, and existing in huge shoals swimming at night, just under the surface. They were known in the town as 'silver darlings'. A settlement based on herring fishing was established in the tenth century, but rapidly expanded after the Norman conquest of 1066.

PH

The boats used to catch herrings were drifters. Their nets floated just under the surface, like tennis nets, with floats at the top and weights at the bottom. The vessel drifted slowly backwards, keeping the nets taut. The nets could be several miles in length, but are now regulated by the United Nations. The herring would swim into them during the night, become caught by their gills, and the haul would be landed on Great Yarmouth quayside in the morning. Great fleets of drifters would follow the shoals down the eastern coast from northern Scotland, reaching Yarmouth in October.

Fish girls from around the country, and especially Scotland, would follow the fleets down the coast, and gut and process the fish. Yarmouth boasted the largest drifter fleet in the UK, numbering over 1,000 vessels, and employing 100,000 fishermen. However, the stocks were overfished, and the herring fishing came to an end during the mid-1950s.

Great Yarmouth was famous for *red herrings*. This was the colloquial name for smoked herring – bloaters and kippers. Bloaters are lightly salted and smoked for a relatively short time, whereas kippers are more heavily salted and smoked overnight. Bloaters especially were associated with Yarmouth, whereas kippers were more widely available.

"Good evening, Lord Nelson", said a youngish couple, chuckling as they passed arm in arm. It was late evening, and I was standing on the promenade at Caister, just north of Yarmouth, where my parents had rented a large, fixed caravan for a week's holiday one August in the late 1950s. I was around five feet tall, and the telescope about four feet long; what a striking silhouette against the background of moon-bleached dunes. The telescope was inexpensive, constructed from a cardboard-like material, but BIG. As darkness fell, I would gaze out to sea, scanning the horizon, and fixing on the flashing beams of lightships. Crowds were still to-ing and fro-ing between the thousands of caravans that were their homes for the week, and the shows at the theatres in Yarmouth, less than a mile or so to the south. There were Nelson-type comments every evening.

Life was generally more leisurely, and so were our holidays. There were no mobile phones, electronic games or laptop computers. It would be two further decades before the Mediterranean package holiday really took off, and the stress of airports, queuing, security, and waiting, waiting, waiting replaced fish and chips in a newspaper, followed by an evening stroll along the prom, before retiring to the caravan for a cuppa before bed. Or maybe a pint.

The odour of Calor gas was a little stifling; it was distinctive, and it was always there. On a few occasions since, I have sniffed it in the air, and immediately been back in that caravan on the North Denes site. But Calor gas was an integral part of a caravan holiday in those days. My sister liked donkey rides, and I wanted to ride in the horse-drawn carriages that took holidaymakers from the Britannia pier to the Pleasure Beach and back.

"Far too expensive", said my father. Donkey rides were more reasonable.

"The Beverley Sisters are on at the Britannia Theatre", said mother. "We've all seen them on the television, but now we will see them properly. On stage. Daddy's booked." And my sister and I knew that they were called Joy, Teddie and Babs, because children of our age learnt things like that. Other celebrities who were household names were on stage, and we saw a few during those summer beach holidays. Charlie Chester and Tommy Trinder's faces on posters still come to mind decades on.

****

"Where did you go on your honeymoon?" I asked one of my staff. I had recently taken Tracey on as a dental nurse, and she had been chatting in the staff room about her recent wedding.
"We went to Hemsby," she replied, with an intonation suggesting that Hemsby was where you *went* if you married in Norwich. Surely I knew that? And indeed, so many local people married, and then drove the twenty miles to Hemsby, and honeymooned in one of the innumerable caravans in those interminable caravan parks packed tightly together, along that part of the Norfolk coast, around seven miles north of Great Yarmouth.

BL

"Was it a good honeymoon?" I enquired.

109

"No. We argued a lot, and it was boring, so we came home after three days," was the sad response. That was in the 1980s.

But Hemsby had not always been wall to wall, shoulder to shoulder, dune to dune caravans. Reflecting on that conversation, I cast my mind back to the late 1950s, when my parents had rented a bungalow there, situated almost on the seashore, for our summer beach holiday. I was around thirteen, and loved that week in the sun, paddling, swimming, and chasing my younger sister across the sand dunes. I had bought a toy Luger pistol which fired quite hard plastic pellets. Poor Julia - she could have wished for a more considerate brother at times.

Perhaps there were caravans tucked away, out of sight. But the Hemsby I enjoyed that summer was a lane going down to the beach, with decently spaced bungalows, and few people and even less cars. It was rural, coastal Norfolk, whereas now it appears to be urban metal and glass, row upon row. And maybe today, within those 'vans, there are still couples honeymooning, arguing, and returning early.

There were low sand cliffs and windswept dunes. The latter were covered with marram grass, also known as beachgrass. The roots hold the sand together, and allow other plants to colonise. But the blades of grass are deceptively sharp, and my sister and I were told to be careful not to touch them. However, most of us sustained some cuts in our hands, and a further memory of Hemsby is – sharply stinging hands when swimming in the salt water of the sea.

We sat on the beach as a family. Adults had deckchairs, and children sat on a rug. We were so often caked in sand, and even sitting on the rug could bring disapproving glances. Norfolk is probably the driest part of the U.K. statistically. Our sky is always blue, in my memories at least, whilst much of the rest of the country sits under cloud cover. But we also have winds that reputedly come straight from the arctic. "Not from the arctic," one old boy informed me. "Norfolk wind comes straight from the Siberian steppes." I would not want to argue that issue either way, but you get the picture. The wind can be cold, and especially if it hails (forgive the pun) from the east. And so windbreaks are a common sight on Norfolk beaches. We had one, and in those days, a mallet with which to hammer it in.

"Has anyone seen Grandpa?" asked my father. What a treat that Nana and Grandpa from Peterborough had joined us again. Grandpa was walking a little more slowly than he had in the earlier Gorleston holiday, and he would take short cuts to the beach by way of paths in the dunes - and get lost.

"He left the bungalow before I did," said Nana. "So he should be here."

My parents were concerned and decided to set out searching for him, when around two hundred yards to the south, we spotted a lone figure on the cliff top, wearing a Panama hat and gazing out to sea. Or was he looking for us on the wrong part of the beach. Waving and shouting was unsuccessful, but father brought him back twenty minutes or so later. He was a lovely man, and that was another precious memory of him.

****

"Mr. Billy Butlin has said that he expects people staying at his holiday camps to spend as much money there as they do in actually paying *for* the holiday," my father announced, having read an interview with the South African-born British entrepreneur. His full name was Sir William Heygate Edmund Colborne Butlin MBE, and the name 'Butlin' became almost synonymous with the British holiday camp, which was aimed at providing an affordable package of accommodation, full board, and entertainment for British holiday-makers. They were situated on the coast, but few people left the camps to reach the beach. My parents were smitten with the camps, and we ventured out of the county, spending two holidays at the Clacton camp in Essex, and two at Skegness in Lincolnshire. There were none in Norfolk.

Our final beach holiday was spent at Brighton, on the distant south coast. I was seventeen, and was not interested in sand or sea, and have few memories of that time. Except Dieppe. My father had been in France and Belgium during World War 2, but neither my mother, sister nor I had ever been out of the U.K. So father arranged a special treat, and we drove to Newhaven and took the sea ferry to Dieppe in Northern France. It was a day-trip, and passports were, thankfully, not required. We explored the town, and the other three each bought a souvenir. Was I indecisive, or was there really nothing that appealed to me? But my budget was small. The time to embark was getting close, and my parents were breathing down my neck. "Get a souvenir, Barrie. You really ought to take something back from France."
And then I saw a sign, and I knew exactly what I would buy and take home as a memento of Dieppe. *Coiffeur*. That was it. I wanted a haircut. A French haircut. I would take it home and everybody would see it. So I dived into the Coiffeur's and explained, "Pour moi" (but who else would it be for?), and twenty minutes later was racing along to the ferry, and back to Angleterre – a Norfolk lad sporting a French haircut.

****

Those times were special. They were family. They were British and they were Norfolk. Buckets, spades, guest houses, caravans, donkey rides, Punch and Judy, paddling, model yachts, seaside shows, sand in our hair, watching the boats come in with Daddy - and Mr. Tennyson's nose. Absolutely unforgettable.

Norfolk holidays – enjoyed under a big blue sky.

 BL

Chapter Seven

Kicking Leaves

The open air - autumn leaves, winter snow, wild mice in my pockets, tracking coypus.

Kicking leaves. Do all three-year-old country kids kick leaves in the autumn? Mother held my hand until the temptation was just too much. I broke free, scampered off, and with total abandon, kicked leaves. That was over seventy years ago, but I can still recall the rich autumnal colours and musky redolence of the carpet of leaves while walking country lanes with my mother. Three years old, and without a care in the world. Kicking leaves.

Maybe we view the past through rose-tinted spectacles, and perhaps we do well to do so. My childhood years were full of sunshine and smiling, friendly people. Taking stale bread to the village duck pond was another adventure during those very early years, and it was always under a cloudless blue sky. The high street was lined with an assortment of quaint olde-worlde cottages, differing roof lines, tiles and thatch, a small number of well-proportioned houses set back from the road with small well-manicured front lawns and roses, and a few traditional shops. It was a short walk, but aged around three, I took tiny steps and was easily distracted. People would greet my mother and ask how old I was, before remarking on my hair. "What lovely curly hair you've got, young man," seemed to be the standard conversation piece.

The lane beside our home, *The Retreat*, was known as Mrs. Pigg's Lane. Looking back with the advantage of many years, it was almost certainly *not* really called Mrs. Pigg's Lane, but was referred to in that manner by my parents. Mrs. Pigg, the lady who delivered milk, lived at the far end. And between our home and Mrs. Pigg's farm was a field. Perhaps it was Mrs. Pigg's field. Years before fertilisers were so widely used in agriculture, crop rotation ensured that the soil remained productive. One year I recall so clearly, it was springtime, and the crop was wheat. My mother would take me along the lane, and it was so safe with very few cars on the roads and virtually none on this lane. Occasionally, Mrs. Pigg would drive by with the milk, slowing down to give us a wave and a smile. Even a day can feel like a long time during infancy, birthdays and Christmases seem a lifetime in coming, and wheat grows extremely slowly. But after a long, long time, there was a magical transition from green to glorious gold. On our walks along that lane, I would stand and stare, almost mesmerised by thousands of ears of wheat shimmering in the breeze.

BL

From our back garden, my four-year-old ears could hear a chugging sound, men shouting, and in the air, more than a hint of dust and corn. The lane was unusually busy, and in the late afternoon, we joined other villagers sauntering down to the corn field. A combine-harvester drawn by a tractor made short work of the wheat, reducing it to stubble. The outside of the field had been covered first, and by the time we arrived, the central area

116

was becoming ever smaller as the harvester continued encircling it.

"There goes one!" There was a loud cry as a rabbit emerged from the diminishing cover and ran for its life. Rough looking men with sticks and clubs chased after it. Then another, followed by two or three more. Everybody was shouting. It sounded like a well-attended football match. The atmosphere was electric, and I was thankful not to be a rabbit. And then it was over, and we were all trudging home. But I retained a delightful memory of harvest.

"Elephants! There have been elephants over here," said Mr. Brown, in a slightly lowered voice. "Come and see. That's an elephant's footprint, sure enough. There are often elephants around here at night." The cricket season was upon us, and father was playing for the village team. My attention span was being seriously challenged, even before the first over was concluded. I wandered around, and later in the season, probably kicked leaves. My mother politely and dutifully watched the match, and if father bowled somebody out, hit a run, or managed a catch, would applaud with enthusiasm. Mr. Brown appeared, and spoke briefly with my mother before saying, "Barrie, let's go exploring." He would take me walking around the periphery of the playing field, occasionally stopping, and studying the ground. "No. That's just worn grass," he would say, or "I think there have been moles here, and that's not what I'm looking for." And then, quietly and with a degree of excitement, "Elephants! There have been elephants over here." With the naïvety of childhood, one would never consider that it might be just another area of worn grass, and in my imagination, I was in another world; a world far more interesting than cricket. Thank you, Mr. Brown, for making my father's cricket matches such an amazing adventure.

JW

"I wonder if Cor Blimey is on duty today?" said my father, as we turned into the Avenues in Wroxham, which led down to the broad.

After moving to Wroxham in 1953, one of our first trips was to the local broad. Wroxham Broad is a lake of around eighty-five acres in size. The public could access it by road at just one car park, though boats of various types were continually entering and leaving via two openings from the river Bure.

"That will cost yew two shillings and sixpence," said the car park attendant. He was probably in his late fifties, with ruddy complexion, grey receding hair, and a large stomach enclosed within a fisherman's-type pullover. Or one could simply say, fat and scruffy. And yet he also knew he was a man with authority. My father was horrified.

"And what do I get for that?" my father enquired.
"Cor Blimey. Yew can park yer car 'ere. Yew can voo the broad. Yew can fish if yew hev a loicence," said the man in charge.
"And if we only want to stay half an hour?" responded father.
"Cor Blimey. It's two shillings and sixpence for the rest of the day. *Or* half an hour", was the answer.

So we stayed about five minutes, and returned home. No money changed hands. My father was not amused. But I found a footpath through the woods behind our new home, which led to the Avenues, and I would walk down to the broad. It was around a mile, beside carpets of bluebells in May, and surrounded by birdsong in every season. Later, when I had a bicycle, I would cycle there, take photographs with my Brownie 127 camera, and look for creatures in the water. On returning home, my father would ask, "Was Cor Blimey on duty today?"

As a small child, I had walked with my mother, enjoying the colours and fragrances of the four seasons, picking wild flowers, catching butterflies in a net, and kicking leaves. And then, for my tenth birthday, my parents gave me a bicycle. The world opened up, and I could explore so much further. Wroxham Broad was a ten-minute ride away, and Salhouse Broad less than thirty minutes.

PH

On the way to the latter I would pass 'bluebell hole'. Well, that was the name local people gave to a hollow in a copse adjacent to the road near Salhouse. I remember one May, picking so many bluebells that it was with difficulty that I cycled home with them. Mother was somewhat bemused at being presented with such a huge bouquet, and put them on display in a number of vases. Sadly, they died overnight. They always did.

"We're looking for the Norfolk broads," said some American chaps I met whilst fruit picking in my teens.

They were slightly older than me. "We've heard about your *broads*," they continued, grinning broadly, "and we want to meet them. Please take us to your broads!"

American slang apart (*broad* was American street talk for a loose woman, and rather dated these days) the Norfolk broads were misunderstood by most people until the 1960s. The broads are 63 lakes lying alongside 7 rivers. The rivers are largely navigable, as are thirteen of the broads. They were thought to be natural features of the landscape until investigated by Dr. Joyce Lambert, a botanist and ecologist, who showed by investigating soil samples, that they were artificial, the result of man-made medieval peat diggings, which had flooded as a result of the rise in sea levels. Peat digging was a major industry in Norfolk from the 12th to 14th century. This area, officially the *Broads National Park*, is generally known as the *Norfolk Broads*. Although the region has been popular for boating holidays for more than a century, it is also rich in wildlife, including some species that are rare, or even, endangered.

"Cor, look Mummy. I've caught one of those swallowtails in my butterfly net," I called out from our rear lawn whilst living in Wroxham in the 1950s. I and my friends were unaware of the diminishing number of these beautiful insects, which became virtually extinct in the succeeding years. Now they are protected, nurtured, and increasing in numbers again.

RH

"Listen! That's a butterbump. Can you hair (hear) it," said the ranger on a broads nature trip. He then explained

120

that *butterbump* was the local name for the bittern, a type of heron and one of the rarest breeding birds in the U.K. Its booming mating call can be heard up to two kilometres away.

Another distinctive feature of the broads is the *wherry*. Wherries are sailing vessels, based on a Viking design, and used to transport passengers and cargo across Norfolk for centuries. They are characterised by one huge sail. They too, became virtually 'extinct', but *Albion*, a trading wherry built in 1898 survives, restored, and owned by the *Norfolk Wherry Trust*, and is available today for charter.

"I'll have a *Wherry*, dear," is frequently heard in Norfolk these days. The location is neither river nor broad, but pub or bar. Wherry is a popular beer brewed locally by *Woodfordes Brewery* at Woodbastwick, a small village on the river Bure, between Cockshoot and Salhouse broads. The Norfolk Wherry lives on!

BL

"You shall have a half crown when you can swim 10 strokes," said my maternal grandmother, known to us as 'Nana at Bungay'. She herself loved swimming, and used her boathouse on the river Waveney for swimming, boating and picnicking. She wanted her grandchildren to share her delight of the water. It was early summer 1954.

Summertime, and our nearest river was the Bure, in Norfolk pronounced Burr, which was around five hundred yards walk from our home. Few homes had a television (though that was fast changing), the word computer had not been heard, and except for listening to

121

the radio (called a *wireless* in those days), we entertained ourselves. We would walk to *Caen Meadow*, where local families would cover the bank, whilst children shouted and screamed, splashing in and out of the water. My sister and I each had an inflatable ring under our arms. Julia's was red and black, and mine was blue and yellow. Mother would coach us from the bank, and the day arrived when we started swimming a stroke or two without rings. Julia was the first to receive her half-crown, several days ahead of me. A half-crown (or two shillings and sixpence) is twelve and a half pence in today's currency - but it was equivalent in value to a little over £3 in 1955. And if I had kept that half-crown until today, I would not get much in excess of £1 for it.

"Get off, you little b****rs," rang out from a passing cabin cruiser. A podgy man in shorts, open neck shirt and sailor hat, was shouting angrily. He had his wife take over the helm, and while his two sniggering children watched whilst perched on the roof, he picked up a boat hook and strode to the stern of the vessel. "Off, or I'll bash yer with this," he bellowed. All eyes were on Podge, with his West Midlands accent and puce complexion, as families along the bank stopped talking amongst themselves, and enjoyed the unfolding spectacle on the river. The cruiser towed a dingy, and two young urchins had swum out and hitched a lift on it. Podge was furious, and swore at them. Whilst the spectators on the bank applauded and cheered them on, the lads stuck their tongues out, yelled obscenities back, and tried to clamber into the dingy. Podge could not reach them with the boat hook, and if he had, would probably have been pulled into the water. As the cruiser rounded a bend in the river and vanished, the two young performers swam back to *Caen Meadow*, acclaimed with applause, and waited for the next ride.

But the river was not all that we assumed it to be in those seemingly idyllic days of carefree childhood, splashing in and out of the water. Sewage. Sewage was, at that time, discharged untreated from passing cruisers, and although we usually swam in fairly clean water, there were those who followed in the wake of a passing vessel, and spent the next few days in bed with a fever. "I wonder where he picked that up from," would be the likely response of the parents.

There were other, more sinister dangers along the rivers, and in the broads themselves, which were often no more than a few feet deep.

"Be careful swimming in Norfolk waters, Barrie," said a good friend of mine, years later. Dr. James Hilton was a GP, but also police surgeon for the region. "People drown in these waters every year. *Every* year," he added. Underwater reeds that wrap around the limbs of inexperienced swimmers, often significantly inebriated after an evening in the riverside taverns, resulted in fatalities every summer, especially amongst holidaymakers. "But we all need to be careful," he would warn me. "Make sure your children are aware of this."

And on a lighter note, I was walking along the green by the river Bure at Coltishall recently, where a number of cabin cruisers are moored every day of every summer month. I enjoyed reading their names, inscribed, usually on the stern of the vessel - names which reflect something of the romance and ethereal magic of our eastern lakeland. *Lazy Days, Broadland Melody, Eastern Dream, Gentle Breeze, Passing Wind, Magical Moments...* But there are comedians lurking amongst us in this part of Norfolk. Did you spot the work of one of them amongst the cruisers' names just now?

"Do yer see that house down there, just below us? Now, what I want yer to do is to break as many winders as yer can. Understand?" We were standing together on a hillside, and a couple of hundred yards below us was a rather smart house, with net curtains at the windows, surrounded by well cared for weed-free grass. My companion was shorter and older than me, slightly hunched, with his weather-beaten face adding years to his actual fifty-five. He grinned as he said mischievously, "And I'm going to give yer ten shillings for every pane of glass yer smash. OK?"

Fred Boyle squatted down beside me and fumbled around in his pockets. The effort caused a few grunts, but a minute or two later he stood up, and there on the hillside was a row of golf tees. He produced a bag of golf balls, placed one on each tee, stood back and challenged me. "Go on. Drive them balls through the winders and I'll give yer ten shillings each time yer break one. Honest I will." I was in my mid-teens and full of enthusiasm.

Wham! Missed completely - the ball was still on the tee. Wham - and it shot along the ground for around fifteen yards. Wham - I missed the next one. Another wham, and it hardly fell off the tee, and rolled a few inches. Wham, wham, wham. Fred was grinning like a Cheshire cat as ball after ball made less than fifty yards from the tee.

Many of my relations played golf, and were more than proficient at the game. Grandpa at Bungay had clock golf on his lawn. The numbers from one to twelve were laid out like a clock face around the central hole. "Go round in twenty-four, and I'll give you sixpence," said Grandpa. I did so after a few attempts, and was duly rewarded. "Twenty-three for another sixpence," smiled Grandpa. That took longer, and twenty-two longer still.

After a day or two I might reach eighteen, after which Grandpa would say, "Let's start at twenty-four again." I loved Grandpa, and couldn't have wished for a better rôle model.

I asked him if I could walk round the golf course with him, and be his caddie. He had a trolley for his clubs, and I pulled it along the fairways, and watched Grandpa and his companions play golf.

"Listen to that lark," said Reggie. Grandpa paused, and we listened. I had never heard a lark before. "Do you see it up there?" said Reggie. "It will fly higher and higher, and after a while you will not be able to see it at all. But you will still hear it." I gazed up at the tuneful little speck, getting ever smaller, and finally absorbed into the blue. It was no longer visible, but the tune continued. That was a memorable moment, and today I regularly hear larks on walks from our home, and on heathland near Blakeney in North Norfolk; they have even flown alongside Wendy and me as we have enjoyed sunshine and sea air. And sometimes they are over our heads, singing, ascending, becoming smaller and smaller – and then, just the song. Whenever I hear larks, I am back on the golf course with Grandpa and Reggie, reliving idyllic days of sixty years ago.

"It's time you had lessons," said Grandpa. "I'm going to pay our club professional and coach, Fred Boyle, to get you going." And within a week, I was swinging a club, and hoping to smash the club house windows. But there was an underlying problem.

Later, my father paid for the two of us to join Mundesley Golf Club, a nine-hole course that was fifteen minutes drive from our home. My game was not very impressive, and my father decided that he would pay for me to have lessons at Mundesley. Every club had a coach, who had been a professional, and was known as 'the pro'. This caused great mirth amongst most of my school friends, who obviously felt that a 'pro' was something more lurid than a golfer. I had several lessons with the pro at Mundesley, who again was a short, weather-beaten and slightly hunched individual. But there was still that underlying problem that could not be addressed.

Some people are innate musicians. Give them any instrument, and they will usually produce a tune. Likewise, some people are innate ball players. If you throw a ball at them, they will almost certainly catch it, head it, or kick it. But I had that underlying problem; throw a ball at me, and I will try and dodge out of the way - and it will still hit me on the nose. I am not really a ball player. But I enjoy golf; fresh air, exercise, wildlife such as squirrels bouncing around on the neatly mown grass, and deer breaking cover from woods lining the fairway, decent chaps to play with, and the challenge to improve my game. I am very content to be less than mediocre whilst enjoying so many aspects of the game. And I love walking in the fresh Norfolk air under that big blue sky.

BL

"Sorry boys and girls," said the bus driver. "You'll have to get off and walk. Really sorry, but I can't go no further." There were around twenty of us, and we had to walk miles to get home. For me it was four and a half miles; for those in Tunstead, less than a mile; but for the boys and girls from Norwich, it would be a ten-mile

126

trudge. Our school bus had become stuck in a snowdrift. Ahead of us were more drifts, and the snow was driving into our eyes and stinging our faces.

There were no mobile phones. There were no *accurate* weather forecasts. I was thirteen and in my second year at the *Paston School*, with a nine-mile bus ride each way every schoolday. It was late February 1958, and during that particular day, there was increasing excitement in the classroom as we watched the snow fall. And it was laying. And then, half an hour before the bell rang to announce the end of the school day, a prefect arrived and whispered something to the master.

"In view of the inclement weather, you may all go home. Those travelling by bus should go straight to the park from which they leave. Class dismissed." We hurriedly packed our satchels and walked, skidded and slid along white pavements through fast falling large snowflakes to the gathered buses. There were around six or seven modern coaches, and a yellow double decker bus. Ours was the double decker. It was ancient, and occasionally broke down. The girls sat upstairs and the boys down. The bus company employed a man to stand at the foot of the stairs to ensure that none of the boys went upstairs, or girls came down. This was considered necessary in those days. The driver was cautious, as we crept along the main road out of town. We turned off onto a narrower road as we approached the village of Tunstead. The snow was falling quickly and densely, obscuring the fields on either side. But the wind was blowing snow from the fields into the road where it created increasingly large drifts against the hedges. The bus shuddered to a halt, tyres spun, and we lurched forward, only to stop once more. The bus started again, stopped, skidded, wheels spinning, with boys peering through snow encrusted windows. It was so exciting, until it became alarming. Eventually we were told to 'get off and walk'.

So we walked. We walked and we walked. It started as an adventure, but the novelty soon wore off. Before long we were cold, wet and tired. Probably an hour and a half later, a snow-caked band of little ragamuffins arrived at the junction where I left them for home. "See you tomorrow *Snowball*", called out the frozen waifs, probably unaware of the pun concerning my nickname. I continued the remaining two hundred yards to my home.

"Where have you been? What happened to you?" asked my parents, who had clearly been extremely anxious. I told them the story, and mother went to run a hot bath for me.
"What's happened to the Norwich boys and girls." asked my father. I replied that they had another five or six miles to go, and were last seen heading in the direction of the city.
"They *cannot* walk all the way to Norwich in *this*," he exclaimed. And what followed must have been one of his greatest acts of self-sacrificial kindness. He walked briskly out of the house, and we heard the Morris Ten (with a Twelve engine – see chapter eight) drive slowly out of the drive and away. I enjoyed the hot bath and came downstairs in my dressing gown, where I was given hot tomato soup for my supper. We waited for father, and waited. We were worried, but could do nothing. And then, the door opened, and a creature looking rather like sketches I had seen of the abominable snowman, or Yeti, stomped into the hallway. "I'll never do a good turn again," said the snowman. "Never, ever."
"Dick, where's the car?" enquired my mother. And he explained that he had soon found five snow-clad children plodding through the drifts towards Norwich, picked

them up, and delivered each to their respective homes. But the falling snow was relentless, resulting in a fateful skid a mile or so from home. The car was abandoned in a ditch, and father had been the one to walk the rest of the way home. So my mother filled the bath with hot water for a second time, and later administered more of her cure-all tomato soup. My sister and I smiled at each other at the "I'll never ever do a good turn again" exclamation - but I still admire my father for his kindness to the children left to trudge home through five or six miles of snow.

Many years later, in my late sixties, I was at our Old Pastonians Annual Dinner, and realised that the man opposite me looked strangely familiar. His face was mischievous, and without knowing him, I realised that he could be a comedian. But maybe I *had* known him. I enquired which years he had been at the school, and he was clearly in the year above me. He now lived in Japan - but where had he lived during his schooldays? And suddenly there was recognition, as his face lit up. "The name's Manning. David Manning. Your father drove me home through the snow one evening. I'll never forget it. What a journey". And I reminded him what had happened to father on the way home, and that he would never forget it either. Surely it was father's finest hour.

BL

Again, it was winter, some years later, and once more the landscape was a refreshing white. We had cycled, and now we walked. Stealthily. We followed the tracks through the snow. It was four-footed, and quite heavy. Not as heavy as a deer, but more than a rabbit or a hare. We followed those tracks for a mile or two, until they went into a hollow tree lying in the snow. They did not come out the other side. We had it cornered.

Catching live mice with my bare hands was my idea of excitement, adventure and achievement. Well, bare hands the first time, when I was bitten; subsequently, gloved hands. I literally fell on them as they ran from straw bales, and took them home in my jacket pocket.

PH

The same pocket in which I had brought home a snake, purchased from a school friend for a shilling during morning break. I will spare you the details of the rest of the menagerie housed in cages, pots, aquaria and jars in my bedroom (it's in another chapter), but must mention the coypus.

As everybody knows, the coypu, or swamp beaver, is around 33 inches, or one metre, from the tip of its muzzle to the end of its tail, looks like a giant rat, but is in fact closely related to the capybara, the largest living rodent and a native of South America. Of course you knew that! I was in my mid-teens, and Norfolk was infested with them. They had escaped from a fur farm owned by Philip Tindal-Carill-Worsley at East Carleton in 1937, bred like rabbits, and found themselves very much at home in the banks of the waterways of Broadland, the Norfolk lake district. Sprouting crops were devoured, farmers fell through river banks into subterranean burrows, and old ladies froze with fear at the sight of long yellow teeth snarling at them. They were quite harmless, with an absolute preference for tender young sugar beet sprouts, far more than sinewy old ladies.

As I have mentioned earlier, my passion was wild life and natural history, and part of the school biology course involved dissecting rats. They were white rats, supplied to the school, probably through the local education authority. Until the supply dried up. No more rats. But I needed rats, to dissect, and from which to learn, in order to pass my biology exams in the hope that I might go on to become a dentist one day. (Why did a prospective dentist need to cut up white rats? A simple question with a very complicated answer. Don't go there). But a friend of mine had the answer to the shortage of rats, and it sounded like an adventure. Even more exciting than mousing. We could track coypus through the water meadows at nearby Tuttington. My friend John had gin traps with which we could trap them. (Gin traps were illegal, but try and tell an adventure-hungry Norfolk lad that). We could take them to the biology laboratory, where we would dissect them like white rats. How did we go about it? - you really would not want to know. The project involved cycling miles and miles over many months, and walking along river banks and across innumerable water-meadows. And before too long, our somewhat bemused biology master stared incredulously as my friend John and I sat there, with huge rodents on the worktops, dissecting, examining, and taking notes that would prepare us for our future professional careers.

And so back to the tracks through the snow. We had cycled to Tuttington, our noses frozen in the cold breeze, and crunched our way across bleak, snow covered water-meadows, where the tips of the highest grass tufts just showed above the undulating carpet of snow. The fallen tree was adjacent to a small copse, the naked trees generously clothed with snow. But our eyes were now riveted on the fallen trunk, and the single set of tracks. Surely it was a coypu. I stationed myself at the hole in the fallen tree where the trail entered, and my friend John stuck his stick under the end where we felt the creature (if there was a creature, and if it was there) would be residing. *GROWL!* Most certainly, there was a creature in the hollow tree. I took up position by the entrance hole, and John started poking the other end. I will spare you further details, except to say that another coypu found its way into our biology lab.

JW

Today there are no coypus in Norfolk. Following their 1937 escape from the fur farm at East Carleton, coypus had spread throughout East Anglia over a period of around fifty years, and were classed as vermin because of the damage to crops. The damage eventually became so expensive that the government set up an independent Coypu Strategy group, and in 1981, twenty-four trappers were employed to clear the region. They used cages baited with carrots, disposed of thousands of the rodents, and completed the task well within the planned ten years. The total cost was over £2.5 million.

****

The Norfolk sky is big because the landscape is relatively flat. From an early age I walked, ran, cycled, swam, caught mice, trapped coypu, played golf, chased girls, kicked leaves and followed scores of other pursuits, under big skies. I'm a 'cup half full' chap, and most of my childhood memories involve big blue skies. My father sometimes used to complain that there was rain most weekends, and bank holidays; he noticed, because those were the days he worked in our garden, or played golf. But I really cannot remember those times; to me, the skies were blue. No clouds.

During that childhood I walked and walked. In my teens, I walked some more. Footpaths, bridleways, water-meadows, golf courses, and usually under that expansive cobalt dome. And then five years in the urban jungle of our capital metropolis, during which I escaped just once to the English Lake District in the counties then known as Cumberland and Westmoreland, and now Cumbria. What breathtaking beauty for a Norfolk lad to behold. Then, a further five years practising as a dental surgeon in Dorset, with its rolling hills and echoes of Hardy. Returning to my native Norfolk, I found myself walking ever increasingly. An annual excursion to Cumbria, and twice-yearly visits to Dovedale in Derbyshire, give us a different perspective on life, as we clamber with aching calves. But Norfolk is home, with its spectacular coastline in the north, and unique network of trails, paths and bridleways through this area of outstanding beauty.

BL

For those interested in exploring an area on foot today, Norfolk has much to offer. The north Norfolk coast is quite distinctive, with numerous nature reserves, salt marshes, seal colonies and the Deep History Coast that is rich in fossils. The oldest and largest mammoth skeleton ever found in the UK was unearthed at West Runton, and at Happisburgh we have the oldest archeological site in Northern Europe.

The broads have already had more than a mention in this book. They are probably best explored out of season, and can be enjoyed on the water, by bicycle or on foot. There are guide books galore, and of course, the Internet.

In the south-west of the county is the largest lowland forest in the U.K., Thetford forest. Planted by the Forestry Commission just after the First World War, it is mainly pine and covers around 20,000 hectares. In addition to hiking and cycling paths, there are a number of commercial attractions. But Wendy and I just love to walk.

To the west of the county is Breckland; wild gorse-covered sandy heathland and one of the driest parts of the U.K. Flora and fauna are protected, and Grimes Graves is the site of a Prehistoric flint mine.

For the hiker, whether serious or fair-weather (Wendy and I are the latter), there are lanes, footpaths, bridleways and ancient walks, such as Weavers Way, Peddars Way, Marriott's Way, the North Norfolk coastal path, and Wherryman's Way, criss-crossing this most delightful of counties. We love walking Norfolk; it might be a fifteen-mile meander using paths and lanes from our home, along Granny Bard's Lane, by Fiddler's Loke and Burntwood Lane – picturesque tree-lined winding rural thoroughfares with quaint names, or along the bank of the river Bure, and back through the hamlet of Little Hautbois (surely of Huegenot origin). One day we will explore two lanes, each a short drive from our home, and whose names express the very essence of rural Norfolk – Muck Lane and Nowhere Lane. And occasionally during the winter months, a moonlit or torchlit night walk of one mile to the *White Horse Public House* and restaurant at Crostwick for a roast beef dinner, (or paella, or curry, or one of a thousand other dishes – a truly amazing menu), a pint and home again. Or, if we feel like two miles, the

Recruiting Sergeant gastropub at Horstead, where the menu is quite outstanding. And even in my late seventies, there are times when the child in me re-awakens, and with total abandon, I find myself kicking leaves.

PH

Chapter Eight

Horseless Carriages

Seven snorting horses, the fire, the salute, and the Pathfinder.

Seven horses were pulling us along, and they were going flat out. We were in an open carriage, to which they were harnessed. The steeds were galloping furiously, and snorting loudly. It was apocalyptic - except I knew nothing about the Apocalypse.

My imagination could be quite vivid at the age of eight, and we had just moved to the Norfolk village of Wroxham. The furniture had been loaded into a *Pickfords* lorry (my maternal grandfather had some interest in *Pickfords*, and any member of the family moving house *had* to use *Pickfords*), together with innumerable boxes and cases into which were packed the entire contents of our home. We had followed in my father's car, an Austin 7.

"Daddy. Why is our car called an Austin 7?" I had asked on what seemed like a really long journey. Well, it was probably around two hours, which was a very long way at my age. It was also a very long way in an Austin 7. My father explained that our car was deemed to be as powerful as seven horses. I sat in the back with my younger sister, daydreaming. Seven horses were pulling us along, and they were going flat out. And snorting.

BL

137

The term horsepower was introduced well before the invention of the motor car. How powerful was an engine? How could it be defined? The development of the steam engine led to a comparison with horses. How many times could a horse turn a mill wheel in an hour? And how did any given steam engine compare? Twice as many times was two horsepower. Three times as many was three horsepower, and so on. What weights could a pony lift? And a horse was deemed to be 50% more powerful than a pony. And again, how did steam engines compare? Later, internal combustion engines. (At school, one of our form masters always called them *infernal* combustion engines. More schoolboy humour).

The first steam-powered automobile may have been invented in 1769, but in 1803 an internal combustion engine powered a car. Later, Karl Benz' petrol powered motor car in 1885 was considered to be the first production vehicle. In October 1908, the Ford model T was developed, and became the first mass produced vehicle. Between 1913 and 1927 over 15,000,000 Ford model T's were sold.

In the UK in 1923, when my father was 10, there were 383,525 cars on the roads. One of them was owned by my maternal grandfather. In 2020, there were 38,800,000. And so, for every car on the road in 1923, there were 100 in 2020. My father was something of an adventurer as a young man, and I can imagine him dreaming that maybe, just possibly, one day he himself would own a car. Whilst at school, he had the opportunity to have a flight in an aeroplane. That was relatively early for a lad whose father worked on the railways, to take to the air. He told me that he and the other boys sat on the floor of the aircraft, and that it bumped a lot. Did they really? Did it really? Although my father was renowned as a teller of tall stories, I suspect his account of that early flight might have been true. My Aunt Marie, his sister, told me that he was 'quite a lad' as a young man, and when his girlfriend, who was French, returned to France, he lost no time in taking the Dover ferry and catching up with her. But later, he met my mother, when they worked together in *Barclays Bank* in Cambridge. They married, and after some years, they settled in Norfolk. However, he had bought his first car towards the autumn of 1946 when I was just two. It was a Riley 9, and a dream come true.

Nine horses flat out and snorting. That was quite a powerful motor car in the late 1940s. These days I drive a car with the equivalent of five hundred and fifty-two horses pulling me. 552 - that would make an interesting picture. The Riley was a beautiful car, oozing character, with a long bonnet. I still have a photograph of it parked outside our home at that time, *The Retreat*, which, covered in Virginia creeper, made a fabulous backdrop.

It was outside *The Retreat* that I would sit on a stool, indulging in a pastime that was not uncommon amongst young boys in the late 1940s, but which would be regarded as a joke today. In my left hand was a small notebook, and in my right a ballpoint pen. The pen was made by *Biro*. Just about all ballpoint pens were made by *Biro*, and most people referred to them as *biros*. In fact, ballpoint pens were referred to as *biros* long after a multitude of other companies produced them. Also, around that time, carpet sweepers were being replaced by vacuum cleaners made by *Hoover*. So vacuum cleaners were called *hoovers*. And again, long after many other companies produced them, housewives used *hoovers* regardless of the brand.

So the little curly-haired boy sat outside his home in the village high street waiting, waiting, waiting. Eventually, there would be the distant drone of a car approaching, and the notebook would be opened, and the *biro* uncapped and ready. As a black motor car approached, I would scrutinise the front, and scribble the registration number into the notebook. And then I would sit back and wait for another. And in those days, it could be quite a long wait. Some readers might wonder if I am serious, but yes – we used to collect car numbers.

My father loved his Riley 9, and I think my mother felt a little like the queen sitting beside him in the front passenger seat. But the car caught fire. And so did my father. He was in his mid-thirties, and my mother eight years younger. In addition to working in the bank, he was starting a small business in photography. Few people possessed a camera in those days, but my father had acquired one abroad, just after the war. He would take photographs of people's homes, and then develop and print them in a darkroom at the back of the house. One shilling (equivalent to 5p since 1971) per photograph was the asking price. They were displayed in the baker's shop across the lane from our home, with the baker taking a small commission. People in the village were amazed to see a photograph of their home, and they sold well. Until everybody had a photograph of their home. But it was the fire that brought the business to an abrupt halt.

He was also forming a company with a Belgian friend called George, which they hoped would profitably produce munitions. It was a very hush-hush affair, and I only realised the nature of the business after my father passed away in 2007, and I was clearing out papers. There were professional diagrams and plans concerning bullets and projectiles. But that project too ended with the fire.

Cricket, football, tennis and golf were other pursuits that enriched my father's life. Dick, as he was known to everyone, was a natural sportsman, and excelled at anything involving a ball. Until the fire.

The Riley was my father's pride and joy. It gleamed as it stood in front of our home. Any speck of dust or splash of insect would quickly be removed. It was regularly washed and polished, inside and out. And all was well until he decided to polish the engine under the bonnet. Apparently he was removing dirt, dust, grease and corrosion with a metal brush, when... BANG! The brush shorted two terminals and the resulting sparks ignited petrol.

JW

He did well to escape with his life, but emerged from the garage screaming, and with his clothes on fire. I feel that his passion for the beloved Riley was greater than life itself, as he ran to the outside tap, filled a bucket with water, and ran back towards the garage intending to throw it over the car. The explosion and screaming caused my mother to run to the dining-room window, gasp and fly out of the back door. Aged four, I peered through the window and observed my father and mother wrestling with a bucket of water, while smoke ascended from father. He was shouting that he needed to put the car fire out, and my mother was screaming "Dick! Dick!" and trying to pour the water over him. The stench of the fire stayed in my memory for decades, and there were times when smelling smoke of a certain type took me back to the dining room window, staring out at that frightening spectacle. A fire engine arrived and took care of the car and garage fire, and an ambulance took father to hospital.

My father was very badly burned, and penicillin was the new wonder drug. But there was no awareness of penicillin allergy, and after the ointments and creams containing the antibiotic were applied to the burnt areas, my father had a second life-threatening experience. Our wonderful National Health Service brought him through, and following a significant stay in hospital, he arrived back home, had a complete nervous breakdown and was unable to leave the house for weeks. But the incident was life-changing, and my father was no longer the adventurous extrovert he had been before. Another result - there was no longer a Riley 9 in the garage, but an Austin 7.

The Austin 7 was described as an 'economy car', nicknamed the 'Baby Austin', and in the U.K. was the equivalent of the Model T Ford in the USA. It was produced from 1923 to 1939, and so our car was at least ten years old in 1949. It was not uncommon to see a car on the side of the road with its bonnet up. It had broken down - and often it was us. And so my father joined the AA, an abbreviation of *Automobile Association*. Members received a handbook to the U.K., a stainless steel and yellow enamel badge emblazoned with 'AA' to fix to the radiator, and a key. The key opened the door to innumerable AA boxes stationed alongside the roads of the UK at intervals of several miles. Each contained a telephone. When you broke down, you could call for help. But for many, the greatest bonus of being a member of the AA was something of a far more fleeting nature.

"AA man!" shouted my father excitedly. My sister and I jumped up and leant forwards between mother and father (there were no seats belts, front or rear, in those days), seething with unabated anticipation. He was coming closer, and four pairs of eyes were riveted on him. And then it happened - taking his right hand from the handlebar, he raised it to his forehead and gave a smart military-style salute. My father acknowledged with a restrained, dignified, partially raised hand, like a general to a private on sentry duty, and mother would give a demure smile. My sister and I would be bouncing with delight, and then impatiently wait for the next one.

On a forty-mile drive, we would usually see two. Each was riding a yellow motor-bike, with a sidecar containing spare engine parts, and all the tools necessary for a motor mechanic. They always saluted, as that was part of the deal. I can also remember the Austin 7 breaking down at Six Mile Bottom. (Six Mile Bottom is a hamlet not too far from Cambridge. It is so named because it is six miles from Newmarket racecourse, and is situated in the bottom of a valley).

"Blast!" said father. "The engine's died. Just won't start again."
"Don't swear in front of the children, Dick," my mother said hastily. 'Blast' was the expletive used if something really went wrong. But when something was especially annoying, the word might move up a grade to 'Damn'. That was the strongest word we ever heard in our home.
"Dash, then," responded father. 'Dash' was considered acceptable, and probably indicated a horizontal line to replace a word that should not be written. Or uttered. Like the swear word 'Blast'. Times have changed.

We were on our way home from seeing my paternal grandparents in Peterborough, and I had been shopping and bought a *Dinky Toy*. It was a die cast truck, and as my parents waited for the AA man to arrive and get us going again, I sat on the roadside happily transporting pebbles to and fro in my little truck. And when the AA man arrived, the occasion became memorable. He pointed to his ears and shook his head, and then pointed to his mouth and shook it again. Pulling a pencil and notebook out of his pocket, he handed them to my father. The patrolman was deaf and dumb, but within thirty minutes, he had resolved the problem and we were on our way home.

Excitement! The Austin 7 was rattling and shaking and felt as though it was about to take off. My sister Julia and I realised that father was really putting the car through its paces. Holding tightly onto the back of the front seats, we leaned forward and gazed at the speedometer. This was indeed scary - we were touching on 40 mph. We gasped - this vehicle could really move. 'Go, Daddy, go!'

It was the same Austin 7, registration ADV 375, in which we arrived at our new home in Wroxham, back in 1953. Of all my father's cars, this was the one that takes prime position in my memory. Seemingly interminable journeys to hospital and back following father's accident and breakdown, and to both maternal and paternal grandparents, were boring beyond belief. It was hot in the summer and cold in the winter. Air conditioning? Heater? This was 1953, and this was an Austin 7.

Our home in Wroxham was an end-terrace house. The unmade road sloped quite steeply in places down to the five-barred gate, and beyond that was our drive and garden. The soak-away for the near white-water rivulets running down the road following a cloud burst, was in our front garden. And after an extreme electric storm, our entire front garden and drive could be located somewhere under the hugely enlarged soak-away.

My parents had kept chickens since my earliest memories, and with their new home, they inherited an eclectic assortment of outbuildings. A brick and tile workshop and log store, sheds, stables and an outside loo. One stable was soon adapted to accommodate the twenty to thirty hens that provided breakfasts and Sunday lunch. Other buildings, even though a trifle dilapidated, were advertised as garages for rent. A few people had motor cars in our area in the early 1950s, but houses had not been built with any concept of car or garage. And so two or three vehicles would drive through our wide gateway and park in the stables overnight. One belonged to Harry Westbury.

Playing cowboys and Indians in the woods behind our home with friends, including Robert the Rough, involved us adopting the names of characters familiar to us from television. Only a minority of households owned a TV, but children of my age would be invited to watch friends' televisions, and over a very few years, most homes did have one. Our first set was brought home by my father in 1955. It was a twelve-inch *Bush*, with a black and white picture. From that day on, we played fewer board and card games as a family, spoke to each other less, but sat in a close circle, squinting at the flickering screen. And on that screen appeared cowboys such as the *Range Rider* and the *Cisco Kid*, and Indians such as *Hiawatha*, and the character known as the *Pathfinder*. We would run through the woods, firing toy revolvers at one another, shouting out "Bang! You're dead," to one another, and "If you ain't being dead, I'm not playing anymore", and go home in a sulk. And so back to Harry Westbury.

He was retired, and lived in one of the small semi-detached bungalows at the top of the road. He was probably in his sixties ('Really old', was how I would have described him), and of average height and average build, but probably balding under that cloth cap, and sporting an untidy moustache that had no doubt seen better days. No-one knew what he had done for a living, or anything else much about him - except for the way he drove his car. Harry trembled not a little, and his hands actually shook. So the steering wheel wobbled, resulting in the car's front wheels wobbling too. The overall effect of this was that Harry regularly hit the pavement kerb along the edge of the road. And this resulted in his nickname - the *Pathfinder*. My father thought it was hilarious, and even at my young age, I could see the joke. So we had a *Pathfinder* on a television programme, played out by me with Roger the Rough and friends in the woods, and Harry was driving around Wroxham, hitting the path beside the road, and also known as *The Pathfinder*.

PH

Whilst living in Wroxham, my father had a second nervous breakdown. Life went on, but the Austin 7 departed. For a while we were without a car, but there were buses, and we had legs. And then father was back working in the bank, and a Morris Ten stood outside our front door. At night it lived in a stable, but my memory only sees it on the drive.

"Got a new car Dick?" neighbours would enquire. "It's a Morris Ten," my father would reply. And then he would add, "But it has a Twelve engine. It really moves".

I heard that description many times, and before long I would be telling school friends, "We've got a new car. It's a Morris Ten - but it's got a Twelve engine. It really moves." I had no idea what that meant, am no petrolhead, and having read a brief history of Morris cars, am still somewhat in the dark. But my father and I spoke of that car with pride. It had a Twelve engine, it really moved, and was powered by the equivalent of twelve horses.

Morris, Austin, Riley, Wolseley, MG, Sunbeam, Hillman, Triumph, Singer, Rover - there were so few cars on the roads when I was a young curly-haired lad, and yet there was a variety of names, the majority of which have been absorbed into the dominant marques of today. We never saw an American car, and there were no Japanese cars. I drooled at the sight of the occasional Jaguar, but did not know what it was. And rarely, there was a Peugeot, though nobody could pronounce it.

Grandpa, who lived just over the county border in Bungay, Suffolk, was the envy of the family because of his cars. My mother could remember him having a 'huge car' when she was quite young. That was in the 1920s. Grandpa and Nana would sit in the front seats, my mother's three siblings on the rear seat, and mother on a stool on the floor. Health and safety? - it would be decades before seat belts were available even for the front seats. And maybe the car appeared 'huge' because my mother was so small at the time. In my teenage years,

Grandpa would drive a Morris Oxford for a year or two before exchanging it for an Austin Cambridge. And then back to a Morris. One had a tasteful green stripe, which was considered very dashing and distinctive, because surely, all normal cars were black. And one day he took me on a business trip to Beccles, around five miles away, touched on 60 mph, but made me promise not to tell Nana.

A new car, larger and no doubt more powerful - more horses - appeared on the drive. Farewell Morris Ten with Twelve engine. And welcome Ford Zephyr Zodiac. The Zephyr was an executive vehicle, and the Zodiac was the luxury version. And with the equivalent of seventy-one horses under the bonnet. When we moved the ten miles to North Walsham in 1958, the Zephyr Zodiac came with us, and on my 17th birthday, I drove it unaccompanied for the first time. When I left for London in 1963, the Zephyr Zodiac was still the family car. It served us well, and to my recollection never broke down in the way that each of its predecessors had. But when I returned on visits home from university, an MG 1100 had replaced the Ford, and I loved it. My father's final car was a Rover. Always referred to as 'the Rover'. Never 'the car'.

Which brings me to a comment reputed to have been made by Jeremy Clarkson, probably on *Top Gear*. "Wherever I go, people point and say, 'Look. There's a Cosworth'. Except Norfolk. There, they point and say, 'Look. There's a car.'"

****

When my father had that first Riley, he was held in awe by many of his peers. To have a car, any car, indicated status, even if it was not acquired as a status symbol. Later, it was the year of registration that was sought after, and especially from the time that letters on the registration, and now numerals, indicated the year. Rolls Royce, I was told as a child, was the vehicle chosen by very important people. The queen always travelled in a Rolls Royce, my mother informed me, in a slightly hushed and very respectful voice; and it was so silent inside that you could hear the clock ticking. Many years later, an uncle told me that they were more usually driven by gangsters.

I prefer to drive a car that is a little distinctive, though never flashy, but have had to settle for very modest vehicles at times. The Reliant Robin caused a few smiles, whereas the rusting Hillman Minx evoked pity. The white Lotus Esprit provoked questions concerning its underwater performance (James Bond fans will understand), whereas most of my friends could not pronounce Lotus Eclat, and some settled for Eclair. In my latter years, I have driven mainly Jaguars, and currently my car, of five hundred and fifty-two horses, has a 'B' monogrammed front and rear. I tell people it stands for Barrie!

Chapter Nine

Cheerful Charlie Rudge

Butterflies, leeches, Tweedledum and Tweedledee, and a faraway honeymoon.

Charlie Rudge was the happiest, most amiable man I had ever met. His eyes twinkled behind his wire-rimmed spectacles, and his large, round, weather-beaten face was just one huge smile. He would lean on his spade, beam at me, with greasy hair falling out from under his grimy, tweedy cap, and say very slowly (because he always spoke extremely slowly), "Are yer awlroight, Barrie boy?" And that big contented smile never left his face.

It was 1961, and I was at grammar school in the Norfolk town of North Walsham. We had moved there from Wroxham, about nine miles away, three years earlier. My parents had taken on Charlie, a jobbing gardener.

I did not think that Charlie could read any faster than he spoke. If he did read. And if he wrote, I suspect that that would have taken a long time too. But why should he ever want to read or write, because he was the very epitome of bliss, just the way he was.

I judged that Charlie was aged somewhere between thirty and fifty, because with some people it is difficult to tell. Chubbiness tends to smooth out wrinkles, and the effects of sun and wind can further confuse the usual indicators. He had been born and bred in the market town of North Walsham, where I had lived for the past three years or so. He may not have been a great academic, but he excelled in contentment. And smiling. That smile was big, just like the rest of him. There are those who describe themselves as big-boned, or having a large frame. But Charlie, our jobbing gardener, was earthy in more ways than one. "Oi do be fat," he volunteered with a fleshy grin. "Oi spose it's them fish 'n chips Oi hev most noights. Love me fish 'n chips." And behind those round, wire-rimmed spectacles, his eyes rolled up and closed as he contemplated the delights of the evening ahead, his empty, greasy plate back in the kitchen as he relaxed in an armchair in front of the telly with mum and dad.

BL

Charlie had what is described as a broad Norfolk accent, as attempted phonetically in the above paragraph. For the rest of this chapter, I shall revert to normal English - but that is not the way you would have heard it.

My parents had always chosen a property with a kitchen garden. My father was a bank clerk, and found his modest income something of a challenge. So the morning call of the rooster, and daytime clucking and scratching, became part of everyday life. I would hear them at first light, and probably much of the neighbourhood would too, though we were not the only garden to house hens in our part of town. However, the Lawrence family enjoyed eggs and chicken meat. And asparagus. Whenever we moved (as bank clerks did regularly), my parents would go into the garden of our new home, and before almost anything else, decide where the asparagus bed would be. And the time came when I would be sick of asparagus, and pray for autumn and the harvest of sprouts. Potatoes, purple sprouting broccoli, cabbage, lettuce, radishes, onions, French beans, broad beans - we were never short of fresh vegetables. And piles of asparagus.

With the passing of time my father attained a degree of seniority in the bank, and an appropriate increase in salary. This led to membership of a nearby golf club, which resulted in less time digging and hoeing. Hence the need for a part-time gardener. Charlie came on recommendation. "He ain't the brightest, but he can dig," said a neighbour. "He don't go too fast, but he gets there in the end. And he's always happy." There was no mention of the rather tepid aroma emanating from the ever-expanding damp patches in the region of the armpits, or the background aura of staleness if one got too close. But we did not get too close.

All the family loved Charlie. In fact, it seemed that all North Walsham loved Charlie. And Charlie loved all North Walsham. He had a smile for everyone, and a few slow pleasantries by way of conversation. Periodically, he would pause from his labour, wipe the perspiration from his forehead with a large red handkerchief, appear to think, and pushing his spade sufficiently far into soft soil, amble over to his bicycle and extract a substantial wadge of sandwiches and a flask of hot tea from his saddlebag. Sitting on the doorstep, or a tree stump, he would smile, indulge, smile again and say, "Good sandwiches these. Love me sandwiches. Mum makes 'em for me."

I thought that cheerful Charlie was so contented, and so set in his casually carefree lifestyle, that he would never ever change. But life is full of surprises, and Charlie was soon to have a big one.

Why was I so fascinated by small creatures? Creepy crawlies and anything that squeaked, hissed, croaked, hopped or wriggled? It started so innocently, and it was probably down to my mother.

"What are those wormy things on the cabbages, Mummy?" I must have enquired, observing caterpillars in our vegetable garden. And so she not only explained that they would later turn into butterflies, but decided to demonstrate. Two or three of the creatures were collected and placed in an empty jam jar. A portion of cabbage leaf was inserted, and the open end of the jar was covered with paper, secured with an elastic band around the neck, and holes punched in the paper. "So that they can breathe", she explained. The cabbage was devoured surprisingly quickly, and frequently replaced. Until, one day, they exuded a silky substance onto a section of cabbage stalk, suspended themselves from their rear end, after which their skin dropped off. The chrysalis that now hung there soon hardened, and my mother explained that inside, the caterpillar was turning into a butterfly. I would go to my jam jar several times a day and peep at them. And one day, there were butterflies in the jar. It was absolutely amazing, and I maintain that attitude today. We released the butterflies, and I would search for other types of caterpillar, feed them with appropriate leaves, and observe the variety of butterfly that emerged. *The Observer's Book of Butterflies* became my favourite tome. In the summer months, I would chase them round our garden with a net, and catch not only peacocks, commas, tortoiseshells and red admirals, but in those days, even the occasional swallowtail.

We would often visit my maternal grandparents at Bungay. Nana and Grandpa had lived in a flat over the family business for many years, before moving into a large house which was only a short walk away. The business was furniture, drapery and haberdashery, and was very successful. The flat consisted of two floors; one where my grandparents and their four children had lived. It was spacious, and even included a large billiard room. Two further stairways led to the second floor, where the children's nanny and two maids had lived. But there was no garden. This deficiency was resolved by purchasing land on the bank of the nearby river Waveney, having a converted railway carriage placed beside the river, and a few other buildings including a boathouse. The family could sleep there, though it was only twenty minutes' walk from their home. I loved that place, was allowed to go there whenever I wanted, and would explore the river and the streams leading into it, using Nana's rowing boat. There were no other boats on that part of the Waveney in those days, and I felt I had found Paradise.

PH

But more exciting still was the abundance of life in and on the water. Sticklebacks are small fish, and could be scooped out of the water with the afore-mentioned butterfly net from one of the three landing stages. I would take them home in a jam jar, and always feel disappointment when they failed to survive overnight. Water snails came in all shapes and sizes, and leeches would creep round the inside of the jar using suction cups at their front and rear ends, attaching first their head to the glass surface, dragging their tail up to it, and then extending forwards again. Creepy. And even more scary, apparently some leeches had ten stomachs, thirty-two brains, nine pairs of testicles and hundreds of teeth. I squinted at length through the lens of my home

155

microscope, but it was cheap and plastic, and I could find no stomachs, brains, testicles or teeth in those I caught in the river Waveney and local ponds. These creatures mesmerised me. Water boatmen and pond skaters were found on the surface, though once in my jar, I could see the boatmen diving whilst holding a bubble of air for their oxygen supply.

The Observer's Book of Pondlife pushed the butterfly edition into second place on my shelf, and the jam jars in my bedroom were to some extent replaced by a large aquarium. Jam jars for the three species of predatory leeches I had collected, and the aquarium for everything else aquatic. Except the frog that lived in a huge jar by my bed, and about which I have written elsewhere. I will not enlarge upon the extent of the menagerie (mother's description), except to say that stick insects, rats, mice and a slow worm were all welcomed and accommodated.

PH

So it was no surprise that the subject that interested me most at school was biology. In the lower forms, those of us who were in the science stream, as opposed to the arts, learnt basic facts about plants and animals. But when I entered the sixth form, I was at first alone in studying zoology and botany. At that time, these subjects were shunned by the other science pupils, and some of those studying the arts actually asked me why I was studying zoos. Bacteriology is the study of bacteria. Egyptology is the study of Egypt. Zoology must be the study of zoos. Was that their logic?

In the upper sixth, there was just one other student in the biology laboratory (a converted butcher's shop adjoining the school property). His name was David Tidy, and at the end of each day, our biology master, John Coward, would say, "Leave the lab tidy," and David Tidy would say, "Yes sir. Immediately!" and walk out of the door and across the courtyard, with Mr. Coward shouting, "Come back Tidy, and don't be so stupid". I spent hours and hours in that laboratory, many of them dissecting rats.

Towards the end of the day, there would be a tap on the door of the lab. "Can I come in, boys?" And there was Hilda, with bucket, broom and dusters. "I can come back later, if you like," she would say, with a broad smile. "Urghhhh! Rats. How 'orrible". Through lenses like the bottoms of milk bottles, she would peer across the lab at the fearsome-looking beasts we were working on. But we were soon to be away, and she would cheerfully flick her duster over worktops and cabinets, and organise her bucket and broom ready for an assault on the floor as soon as we had departed.

She was short and dumpy, early thirties, chatty, and with the hint of the fragrance of floor polish about her. From below her mouth, a succession of chins descended to the region of the larynx. A hair net prevented her mousy locks from falling forward and obscuring the area of floor to be addressed. Happy in her work, she would lean on her broom, smile and ask, "What you boys doing with those rats then?" I would explain that we needed to know what was inside them, because much the same was inside us, and if I wanted to be a dentist... but then the explanation would become rather obscure, and I would revert to, "And what sort of day are you having, Hilda?"

Hilda's days were happy days. She cleaned a few houses during the mornings, and came to the school late afternoon. "Lovely job cleaning," she explained. "A room can be all untidy, even grubby, or cobwebs, and then I come along, and after a while, it's all clean again. Lovely job I've got. Don't know why more people don't do cleaning". And she would lean on her broom, close her eyes, and no doubt daydream for a short while of grime, cobwebs, dust layers, and other aspects of life that she relished. "Life is good," she would say. "You can't beat a bit of cleaning, and I really cannot imagine being happier than I am now."

But life really is full of surprises, and like Charlie, Hilda was soon to have a big one too.

****

From a very early age, my mother would read me stories. This was the age of *Rupert Bear*, *Winnie the Pooh*, and the *Water Babies*. Later I would read by myself and graduate onto the *Famous Five*, the *Secret Seven*, and *Treasure Island*. But in those early days, *Through the Looking Glass* was standard fayre, even for a young lad. The edition my mother used was illustrated, and if there was one picture that stuck in my memory, it was that of Tweedledum and Tweedledee. With a bright splash of colour amongst the standard black and white text stood two figures that closely resembled Toby jugs. Neckless, their outline swept smoothly from their heads to their hugely expanded waistlines, and then equally smoothly down to their feet.

And one day, walking along the high street in North Walsham, there in front of me stood Tweedledum and Tweedledee. But no, for there was a striking difference.

Indeed, whereas Tweedledum and Tweedledee were always arguing, this couple were smiling. Beaming.

"We're in love, Barrie boy", said Charlie, slowly.
"So in love", echoed Hilda.

And so they were. Hopelessly, and irreversibly, in love. As a couple, hand in hand, Tweedledum and Tweedledee, and beaming at everyone and anyone, Charlie and Hilda became a feature in my home town.

Wedding rings appeared on the appropriate fingers, and they set up home in a small terraced cottage in Kings Arms Street. They were inseparable, except when gardening and cleaning. And their honeymoon tales became close to legendary. I enjoyed calling in on them from time to time, and always received a huge welcome.

"Barrie boy, come on in. Love, it's Barrie boy. Put the kettle on Love."

We would exchange pleasantries, and they then enquired how my studies were progressing, and of plans concerning my future. But Charlie's eyes would soon roll up, indicating that he was thinking. And he would recount memories of their honeymoon.

"Me and Hilda, we're Norfolk people, like, really local. Born in North Walsham, we were, both of us. Been to Norwich we have, and seen the shops and market and castle and all that. On the bus. And we been up to

Cromer on the coast. On the bus, of course. Nice pier, and really good fish and chips. But we wanted to get away. Right away. We're Norfolk, and we wanted to do different, like. Wanted to travel, and see more of the world. So, on our honeymoon, we went to Kings Lynn, didn't we Love."

"That we did, my dear. All the way to Kings Lynn. On the bus."

Charlie's eyes rolled up, as he thought back to the adventure of a lifetime.

"They speak different up there, of course," he informed me. "We could understand them, and they could understand us, but they do talk different in that part of the world. You see, they're a different people from us. Much more north they are. It's a lot colder up there, in that part of the world. Always wondered what it was like, but wouldn't want to live there."

He paused, and reflected further on their foray into that distant land.

"Food's different too. I mean, large cod is large cod down here. Well, it's a lot smaller when you go north. To Kings Lynn, like. And the chips aren't quite the same. I thought they were a bit soggy. And so did you, didn't you Love?"

"Yes my dear. A bit soggy. But it was a special time, being on honeymoon, even if it's colder up there, and the chips are soggy. We stayed in a nice guest house, and Mrs. Grubbing did a lovely cooked breakfast each morning. And we would walk round the town, sightseeing. And the people would smile at us. Different, they are, but quite friendly really."

160

In 1963 I left North Walsham and went to London where, for five years, I studied dentistry before moving to Dorset, where I was in practice for the first five years of my professional life. I lost touch with Charlie and Hilda, which on reflection, was a loss. They were Norfolk treasures. The salt of the earth. Totally without guile. Kind, neighbourly, and wanting only to enjoy a quiet life together within a community doing the same.

But that was back in Norfolk in the late 1950's and early 1960's. The county was much more parochial and insular in those days. Before computers, and tablets, and android phones. And the Charlies and Hildas of that era had simple rural charm that is largely, and sadly, missing today.

Real Norfolk characters – I love them.

JW

Chapter Ten

Remote and Insular

Culture shock, the accent, the Canaries, Scottish drovers, Boudicca.

"Excuse me asking, old chap," said a frightfully well-spoken fellow-resident of Commonwealth Hall where I was living in Bloomsbury, a district in central London. "I mean, I'm not too sure where you come from, but has news not reached you yet? The king is dead. Over ten years ago actually. And dare I ask? - do you have horseless carriages where you come from? Mains drainage?" The man was clearly a comedian, but...

****

Norfolk was, and to some extent remains, rather insular both geographically and in its mindset. If we were in the middle of the UK, it would be different. Or even centre top or centre bottom. But we are not; we are a bulge sticking out on the eastern side. "On the roight", as I have heard it explained locally.

If you are travelling to Scotland you might pass through Yorkshire, Tyne and Wear, Durham and Northumberland, or perhaps Derbyshire, Lancashire and Cumbria. But if you pass through Norfolk, you are heading for the North Sea. So you don't pass through Norfolk; you come to Norfolk if that is your destination. And for many centuries, people generally did not come to Norfolk. Indeed, some who did were lost in the marshes

163

and never seen again, so one understands from what are largely legendary tales of Boudicca, Queen of the Icenis.

So, with the accent, and with words that are peculiar to the county, the Norfolkman can be regarded as something of a curiosity when he ventures out of his homeland. And this can result in a degree of unexpected culture shock.

It was the summer of 1963. I had worked on a farm for a few months before going to London to study dentistry. The local accent is particularly strong amongst those working on the land, and my friends and I soon learnt to accentuate our accents in order to fit in. My parents said that at times they could not understand me. "There's nart sich a hooge diffrence that we can't hev a mardle, is there?" I might have asked them. And in case that is a little obscure, I was saying, "There's not such a huge difference that we cannot have a chat, is there?"

It was September 1963, and I was starting my course in dentistry in the East End of London at the London Hospital. It has since become the Royal London Hospital. But I lived in a University hall of residence, called Commonwealth Hall, in Bloomsbury in central London. That hall was boys only (all female guests to be signed out by 10pm) and next door was Canterbury Hall, exclusively girls (and all male guests to be signed out by 10pm). With hindsight, I suspect that my Norfolk accent stood out like a sore thumb, but I was oblivious to it. The excitement of being in London with a great variety of new friends from all over the world, as well as the U.K., was overwhelming. When I spoke about the college *tooters* or mentioned that a girl was *bootiful*, I was largely unaware of the smiles passing between those with whom I was in conversation. When I asked for a *mardle*, they were silent. And then there was the conversation in which I was asked if I knew that the king was dead, and concerning mains drainage.

It was my mother's fault. Well, no fault really, and in fact, it was her sacrificial love for me plus my dialect, which led to this rather comic conversation. There were no mobile phones, or internet in 1963. In fact, there were just two or three payphones between a few hundred students, though they were rarely used. But my mother wrote to me very regularly. There were pigeon holes for mail, and early each week, a letter would arrive from Norfolk, in which my mother would bring me family news, and enquire as to how I was enjoying life in the big city. My parents were not well off financially, and even buying a stamp with which to send the letter, became something of a challenge. So mother had a brain-wave, and started scavenging her stamp collection of many years. King George VI had died in 1952, and Queen Elizabeth II was crowned in 1953. Stamps bore the monarch's head, and from 1953, letters had stamps bearing the head of Elizabeth II. Except for a few arriving in London from Norfolk! My friend, the well-spoken Sebastian Davenport-Jones saw me with such a missive in my hand, and plunged in, questioning whether news of the king's death ten years previously had yet reached Norfolk. My speech may have afforded me the persona of a yokel amongst some of my more sophisticated friends, which was probably the excuse for the further comedy concerning whether the horseless carriage and mains drainage were to be found in the county yet.

Another student asked where I came from. "It's your accent," he explained. "I haven't heard one like that before. But I *can* understand you." Other curious students gathered, and I felt rather embarrassed. Why did they remark on the way I spoke? Maybe my intonation was a little different, but were there not other regional dialects in evidence around the common room in the evenings? I went into defensive mode, with, "Blust! Oi doont hev noo accent, do Oi?" which simply evoked an explosion of uninhibited mirth from my companions. I had heard it said that, if you can't beat them, join them, so I gave a hearty laugh along with them, but beat a hasty retreat to my room, where I sat and thought about the matter. This was not the first time my Norfolk accent had caused me a degree of embarrassment.

BL

Evening dinner at Commonwealth Hall was a reasonably relaxed affair. We would saunter in, queue for a minute or two while our plate was loaded, and then find a place at one of the long tables arranged in rows the breadth of the room. Unless one had been invited to the high table, which only happened periodically. I received my invitation early in the first term, and was told that I would need a gown. The warden and vice-warden, who were professors, accompanied by around ten other academic staff who held doctorates, would have six student residents join them for dinner. We met in an ante-room for pre-dinner sherry, and then entered the dining hall, where everyone paused eating, and stood to their feet until the warden's party was seated. The academics made polite conversation around the table, and the doctor opposite me enquired, "Now, I can tell that you come from some part of our commonwealth. I am correct, am I not?"

I assumed that the U.K. was as much a part of the commonwealth as, say, Australia or Nigeria, and answered in the affirmative.

"Right," said the learnéd gentleman opposite me, "Let me guess. Er, I think you're from..." he paused, "South Africa. Am I correct?"

I told him he was wrong.

"OK, but I'm sure I'm not far out. So how about.. er.... Southern Rhodesia?"

"Wrong again," I responded, just starting to wonder whether I had been a little misleading earlier.

"But I feel I'm close," he continued. "Northern Rhodesia?"

"No".

"Nyasaland?"

"No".

"Kenya?"

"No".

I am not sure who was the more embarrassed as this game of 'Guess Where?' came to a halt, with our fellow diners craning their heads to follow the to-ing and fro-ing of question and answer?

"Sorry. I give up. Where are you from?" enquired Doctor Frustrated-Perplexed.

"Oi come from Narfick". I replied.

"Where?" asked the doctor, looking more than a little irritated.

"Narfick. Jist north arf Narwich".

There were a few smiles from around the table, and the warden looked at Doctor Inquisitor and said, "Oh. He comes from Norfolk. Missed by one thousand miles, or maybe eight, didn't you, old boy," and grinned.

Following that, conversation was quite sparse, especially from the seat opposite me.

And yet, there was an encounter that was unexpected and so different. It had been my very first evening dinner in Commonwealth Hall, and emerging from the service hatch with my plateful, I ran my eye around the room, and knowing absolutely no-one there, made my way to sit opposite a bespectacled, studious-looking guy who was about to start his dinner. "My name's Barrie," I introduced myself.

"Simon", said my fellow-diner.

"Where are you from," I asked Simon.

"You won't have heard of the actual place," said my new friend, "but I come from the county of Norfolk."

"So do I", I retorted excitedly. "Where in Norfolk?"

"Near Norwich," he replied warmly.

"Where near Norwich?" I enquired eagerly.

"Thorpe, on the east", said Simon. I told him I came from North Walsham, and there, with fellow residents from every member of the Commonwealth and further still (Mr. Gan came from the People's Republic of China), we marvelled at the fact that our homes were so few miles apart. Simon was studying nutrition, which was a new subject for students at Queen Elizabeth College, and his father wrote a column in our local newspaper under the pseudonym *Whiffler*, and was a household name in the county. But Simon spoke like a BBC newsreader. Maybe I could lose something of my brogue. Maybe I could flatten it out.

I worked on it. The word was beautiful, not bootiful; huge, and not hooge; I and not Oi; and so on. Fifty years later, my wife tells me that there is little evidence of Norfolk in my speech, except when I'm angry (rarely, if at all) or tired (often). Which leads to a further problem. A few years ago, I was attending an Old Boys Dinner back at the *Paston School*, now sadly a sixth form college, where two of our grandchildren have completed their Norfolk-based education. There were two chaps from my year of 1956-1963, and one of them asked me, accusingly and bordering on aggressively, "Why on earth are you speaking like *that*?" I explained that my accent had caused mirth and embarrassment in London, and so I had tried to flatten it. And the way I spoke now had been part of me for the last half-century, and I was unable and unwilling to change it again.

And then the irony; Norfolk boy spends five years in London, and five years in Dorset, returns to Norfolk and is accused of speaking strangely. Almost properly. How very pecooliar is that?

****

The incident concerning my friend Simon Amies from Thorpe, whom I met quite by chance in the dining hall on my first evening in London, came back to me a few years ago whilst flying from Buenos Aires to Ushuaia in Argentina. Maybe there is an unseen magnetism between Norfolk people, whereby they are unknowingly drawn towards one another.

I have a mission statement for my life. It is short and simple, but I take it seriously and it is important to me. 'I am on this earth to please God, and to make my wife's dreams come true'. Some chaps tell me it makes them feel like throwing up! So when Wendy and I became engaged, I probed to find out what her dreams were. She had been by herself for eighteen years, bringing up two daughters, and working all hours. She watched television when she could, and enjoyed travel programmes. Her top three dreams were to visit certain destinations abroad. She told me that they were just dreams, but I was determined to make them come true. The top two were beyond my wallet, but I managed number three, a Kenyan safari, for our honeymoon. The following year I found a package holiday to the Galápagos Islands, and realised dream number one, and a year later, dream number two, the Great Wall of China. Wendy then asked me about my dreams. I quoted the Old Testament prophet Joel, that 'old men shall dream dreams', but suggested that because I was indeed getting old, perhaps around sixty, I could not recall any. And then I remembered my boyhood fascination with the Antarctic.

So we flew to Buenos Aires, and after a few days boarded a flight to Ushuaia, in the very south of Argentina. We were travelling Economy, and Wendy leant over and whispered in my ear, "Ask the man on your left where he comes from." So I introduced myself, and asked him where he was from.

"Near Cambridge", he informed me.
"Right. Cambridge. Well, I'm from that general area, but I come from Norfolk", I replied.
"I'm from Norfolk too", he said.
"I thought you just said Cambridge". I smiled and added, "But Norfolk?"
"Well, no-one's heard of Norfolk," he explained, "So I say Cambridge. Most people have heard of Cambridge. I actually come from Norwich."
"I live north of Norwich, in a village called Frettenham. I've lived there a long time and enjoy rural Norfolk," I told him.
"I live in a village just north of Norwich, about three miles from you," he said with a grin. "Little Hautbois.

But I say Cambridge because a lot of people have not heard of Norfolk. And I say Norwich because not many people have heard of Little Hautbois."

Little Hautbois – Hautbois is pronounced 'Hobbis', or in the local accent, 'Arbis' - probably owes its name to the Huguenots who fled the inquisition in France during the 1680s. The name is actually spelled 'Hobbis' on a memorial on the outside of nearby Lamas Church.

We boarded a ship in Ushuaia, and sailed to the Falklands, then South Georgia, Coronation Island and down to the Antarctic Peninsula, where we walked with the penguins. Then to the Wedell Sea, and after a few hours, pack ice. About turn, and back via Deception Island and Elephant Island, and Cape Horn where we hit a gale and the vessel sustained damage. Quite an experience, and the *MV Discovery* never sailed to the Antarctic again.

The ship could take around one thousand people, but there were only four hundred on board so that we could each make more excursions to the islands, and Antarctic mainland. We engaged other passengers in conversation, and there was another memorable incident, when we were speaking to a charming Asian couple.

"Where are you from?" I enquired.
"England," they said. "A town called Dereham. In Norfolk. And you?"
"England," I replied. "A village called Frettenham, in Norfolk. About twenty miles from you."

****

171

Norfolk continues to be, to some extent, insular and parochial. We do not expect people to know where Norfolk is. Well, our friend from Little Hautbois felt that way. And so we are careful to help people understand, assuming the accent does not confuse them. Sometimes when abroad I will point to a spot on my hand and say 'London'. Then point up and right, and add, 'one hundred and fifty kilometres. Norwich'. Or, if it is a fellow over the age of eight, and almost anywhere in the world, the words 'Norwich City Football Club' brings tremendous enlightenment, as the waiter in Beijing, or the porter in Nicosia, or the market trader in Delhi comes alive and says, "Ah. Canaries. Premier League (or, sadly, Championship). Yes. Norwich Ceety Football Club."

BL

The Canaries might be known in most parts of the world, but locally they tend to be the butt of many jokes. Here are two. Burglars broke into Carrow Road and completely cleared the trophy room at Norwich City Football Club. Police are searching for a man with a green and yellow carpet.

Here is another. The Football Association have stepped in to prevent the pet food suppliers *Spillers* from sponsoring Norwich City Football Club. They said the club could be accused of fraud if they wore shirts with *Winalot* printed on them!

Within the British Isles, the Irish are often the target of jokes, especially those starting with, 'There was an Englishman, a Scotsman and an Irishman......' Within the county of Norfolk, the town of Kings Lynn seems to figure in a rather unflattering way in a number of jokes. For instance, there is the question, 'What is the difference between a man from Kings Lynn and a coconut? The answer - you can get a drink out of a coconut! Perhaps if I lived further to the north and the west of the county, and nearer to Kings Lynn, I would hear more jokes about Norwich.

And then there's the redeeming manner in which some people can laugh at themselves. Tom Morley, a Norfolk farmer, answers a knock at the door to find two policemen who are investigating the possibility of illegal immigrants working on his farm. They ask him about his workers.

"I have three men work here," says Tom. "There's Fred the shepherd. He works eighty hours a week, I pay him two hundred pounds and include free board and lodgings. There's Jack the cowman. He also works eighty hours a week, and I pay him two hundred and fifty pounds, and include free board and lodgings. And then there's the halfwit. He works around one hundred and twenty hours a week, I give him eighty pounds, and he looks after his own board and lodgings. But I buy him a bottle of Scotch now and again, and - sh," and he grins at the policemen and lowers his voice, "he sometimes pinches my wife on the bum, and I'm sure she really enjoys it!"

"He's the guy," said the more senior policeman. "I would like to speak to your halfwit, Sir."

"Not difficult," said Tom. "You're speaking to him!"

****

I have already stated that people only come to Norfolk if that is their destination. It is not an area that you pass through, unless you are heading for the North Sea. And yet, having said that, a few specific groups have been welcomed into this relatively remote part of England; people who have come with a specific purpose. Scottish drovers brought cattle from the twelfth to the nineteenth century, Flemish weavers came with their particular skills in the sixteenth and seventeenth centuries, holiday-makers really started arriving from the nineteenth century, and today, Eastern Europeans swell the ranks of the summer fruit-pickers.

I shall make reference to the Flemish weavers in chapter twelve. Holiday-makers originally came in the nineteenth century, in very small numbers, to enjoy the broads, though that industry has expanded greatly, especially during the twentieth century. The coastal attractions vary from the unspoilt serenity, seal colonies and bird sanctuaries of north Norfolk, to the summer razzmatazz of Great Yarmouth, and there are inland areas of unique character and beauty described elsewhere in this book.

Every autumn, from the twelfth to the nineteenth centuries, there was another friendly invasion from the north. Cattle were the main source of a Scotsman's wealth in those days, and the beasts reared on hillsides and moorland were small, but hardy. The latter ensured they could make the long trek from south-west Scotland, across the Pennines, and down into Norfolk, where the better quality grazing, straw and root crops enabled the county's farmers to fatten them up. And then to the markets of Norfolk and London, and on to the butchers.

A wealthy Scottish nobleman could send four thousand head of cattle (Galloway was the preferred breed in Norfolk) a year, and around eighty thousand would arrive annually. Horsham St. Faiths is a small village around two miles north of Norwich, and a little over a mile west of my home today. The current population is around fifteen hundred, and yet, from the twelfth to the late nineteenth century, fifty acres of land was used for the St. Faiths Fairstead, a huge cattle fair lasting three weeks from 17th October each year. The area would be heaving with drovers, farmers, spectators, and thousands of head of cattle. The village boasted six public houses, patronised by hundreds of thirsty, ale-drinking drovers. The fair was situated between two lanes, whose names continue to bear witness to their past glory - Calf Lane and Bullock Hill. Today, there is one pub, one small store, and relatively empty fields, where a handful of horses graze. Rural Norfolk, in all its pastoral serenity.

BL

Finally, I mentioned that people of a bygone age could visit Norfolk, but might get lost in the marshes and never return. Let me tell you about Boudicca, Queen of the Icenis.

If Admiral Lord Nelson was Norfolk's greatest hero, Boudicca (or in Latin, Boadicea) was our county's greatest heroine. In fact, this Iron Age warrior queen was a national heroine. Her husband, Prasutagus, was king of the Celtic (though this has recently been questioned, and so possibly Germanic) Iceni who occupied what is now Norfolk (and a small part of northern Suffolk and a trace of north-eastern Cambridgeshire). When the Romans invaded Britain in AD43, he became a client king, and when he died in AD60, left half of his kingdom to the emperor Nero, but the other half to his two daughters. The Romans had expected all of his kingdom to be passed onto them, and reacted to this by looting his palace, stripping Iceni chiefs of their lands, flogging Boudicca and gang-raping his daughters.

Boudicca plotted the Iceni revenge, and whilst the Roman forces were fighting in the west of Britannia, she marched with an army said to be between 100,000 and 200,000 on Camulodunum (Colchester). The Romans were taken by surprise. Thousands, left to defend their capital, were butchered, and the city burned. They then marched on the relatively new Roman city of Londinium (London), a trading centre with a population of around 30,000. Many fled, whilst others were hacked to pieces or skewered on wooden poles, and there were rich pickings for the pillaging Iceni. Next, in the summer of AD60, Boudicca's army marched on Verulamium (St. Albans), the third largest Roman city in Britannia. With no garrison to protect them, the population fled. By this time around 70,000 Roman citizens had been slaughtered, including 1,500 of their crack troops.

The Roman governor Paulinus ceased his campaign in the west, and marched his troops south-east to confront Boudicca's army. At the battle of Watling Street, her forces were devastated. Although history is unclear, it is said she fled back to Norfolk. Pursuing Romans were bogged down in the marshes, and Boudicca committed suicide, taking poison.

It is impossible to distinguish between history, folklore and legend. The two historical accounts, by Tacitus and Dio are Roman, with inevitable bias. They record that Paulinius' disciplined army of 10,000 overcame Boudicca's ragtag mob of 230,000. Historians seriously question the figures - for an army of even 100,000 to march from Norfolk to Camulodunum and on to

Londinium, with no roads and so many mouths to feed, seems unlikely.

But all are agreed that this iconic queen was a fierce and noble warrior. She was reputed to have been a striking looking woman; tall, with red hair tumbling below her waist, a piercing gaze and a harsh voice. One biographer describes her as 'terrifying'. In fact, not too different from a few of the characters I have met in the county during my lifetime.

JW

Chapter Eleven

Normal for Norfolk

Pig on the A11, Grenville, brushes with De'ath, the Tortice family, and Mr. Bean.

There is an expression which has for years been well-known within the county, but which I have recently heard used elsewhere, indicating that we are a little less insular than in the past. *Normal for Norfolk* is probably self-explanatory, and is applied to accounts of various happenings and people. They usually conjure up a picture of rural idiosyncrasies, yokels, or farm animals. For example, Wendy and I sometimes pass a road sign reading *SLOW YOU DOWN*.

JW

Normal for Norfolk is thought to have originally been a derogatory term used by doctors in the county to describe some of their more foolish and ridiculous patients. They would scribble *NfN* on the patient's records to warn any future doctor who might see them.

Actual incidents that might be described as Normal for Norfolk include several miles of tailback on the A11, the main arterial road into Norfolk, due to a pig strolling along the carriageway at Thetford. In February 2016, a tractor thief was jailed for stealing the agricultural vehicle and leading police on a 10 mph chase across the county. Both the above stories were reported in our local award-winning newspaper, the *Eastern Daily Press.*

JW

The suggested medical origin of the *NfN* expression certainly has a very close parallel in my own dental profession. Where a patient was a nuisance, maybe complaining at length about the cost at every visit, or repeatedly arriving late or missing appointments, the abbreviation *pia* was often scribbled on the front of the patient's records. pia? It's short for *pain in the backside*, but in even more colloquial English. The abbreviation was questioned in one or two litigation cases, where the dentist would explain in court, "It's short for 'patient in agony', and ensures that they get seen promptly". But we were rumbled, and several years before I retired, those of us who were members of *Dental Protection*, one of our medico-legal indemnity companies, received a letter warning us that 'courts in the UK will no longer accept that *pia* is an abbreviation for *patient in agony*'. Short and to the point.

"Sugar beet? Where *are* the sugar beet? All I can see are potatoes," said Wendy, looking totally mystified.
"And how can we walk to the left of the hedge like the book says - when there is no hedge?" I added with a sigh of frustration. Norfolk!

We had been looking through the selection of a score or more of Norfolk walks books. They had accumulated over the nearly forty years I have lived in my home, and although I have bought many myself, quite a number have been gifts. Friends and family know that Wendy and I love to walk Norfolk.

One such book was a compilation of walks published by a local newspaper. 'Twenty-Five Rural Walks' or similar was the title. We tried a few, and enjoyed the expansive panoramas under big Norfolk skies, as we meandered along footpaths, field edges, crossing becks and clambering over stiles.

"Pass through gap in hedge, and follow the path towards an oak tree on the skyline," I read out. And as we approached the oak tree, "Then turn diagonally left, and cross a bridge into a wood. Follow the obvious path." It was quite clear, and we followed the directions, until, "Proceed along path, maintaining direction. When you reach a field of sugar beet, take the path walking to the left of the hedge."

And this begged the question, "Where the heck *are* the sugar beet, because all we can see are potatoes? And there is no hedge."
Which in turn caused us to grin at each other and say in unison, "Normal for Norfolk!"

The newspaper had outlined a Norfolk walk every weekend for a number of weeks. Their readers enjoyed them, and had written in to say so. The newspaper had then selected the twenty-five walks they considered the most popular, and published them as 'Twenty-Five Norfolk Walks'. And almost exactly twenty years after publication, we had taken the book off the shelf in my study, blown the dust away, and started walking the walks, until... we discovered that there had been an oversight; farmers harvest crops, and often plant something different the following year. And twenty years later, the sugar beet had gone. Long gone. Potatoes had arrived. Maybe the previous year was barley, and the year before maize. And the hedge had gone too. So we laughed at our experience of Normal for Norfolk, and started guessing the way ahead. Which in this county, is all part of the fun.

****

Our friend Granville is both Norfolk and accident prone. That is a wicked combination. But he never stops laughing, and everybody loves him to bits. I first came across the name Granville when taking the family to a campsite in France one summer. The children young and excited, and we all have wonderful memories of that time, not least of dad firing corks out of bottles of French sparkling wine, and seeing how far they would go. "Hit the cow, dad. Try and hit the cow," from young daughters gazing mischievously into the orchard with cattle adjacent to our site.

It was a short drive to the town of Granville, with its battlements, quaint buildings, historic old town, and views out to sea. And ice-creams. But it was not until I was well into my thirties that I came across a *person* with the name of Granville.

A huge American open-top car resembling a cross between a juke box and a Christmas tree drew up outside my city practice. The young man sitting behind the wheel was deeply tanned, had shades, bleached hair, and a Hawaiian shirt with at least the top three buttons undone.

Chest hair and a large nugget on a gold chain had burst through. Tracey, my nurse, whooped with excitement, and scarcely managed a 'See you after lunch' as she practically fell down the stairs in her enthusiastic dash to the new boyfriend's motor. He was taking her out for lunch.

"Was that a spaceship you sailed off for lunch in?" I enquired later.
"It's American. Really amazing. So powerful and uses loads of petrol. It's Dexter's. He's my new boyfriend. Got oodles of money. Took me to a posh pub for lunch. Scampi and chips," she bubbled out.
"Wow. He sounds fun," I replied. "What does he do for a living?"
"He works with his dad. They mend washing machines. Ever so busy. His dad is Grenville Flashman. He's got a roller what he drives."
"Grenville? That's a new name to me," I said. "Unusual".
"Grenville. "G-R-A-N-V-I-L-L-E," she spelt out. "Grenville."
Of course. Granville, pronounced Grenville. Subtle, and quite Norfolk. As in, "Thet's the way we speak in Norfork."
And that, or thet, was the first human Granville I had heard of, but there were more.

BL

CRASH! We were preparing the church for a Sunday morning service, when there was the sound of chairs falling over, and a great shout. "It's Granville," said my friend Keith. "He said he was coming this morning. Hasn't been before. Incredibly clumsy. He's just tripped over some chairs." Indeed, the new chap at our church was one of the clumsiest people I had met. Six feet tall, with an ungainly walk, and almost continually chuckling away, he knocked things over, walked backwards into people, walked forwards into plate glass doors, and seemed to spend half his time laying on the ground.

Granville was a delivery driver, working for a well-known company, and taking parcels and packages all over Norfolk. Dersingham is a village in north Norfolk, just a stone's throw from the Sandringham estate, the Norfolk rural retreat of the Royal Family. And two miles from Dersingham is an even smaller village called Anmer. It was around Christmas time, and Granville had delivered a number of packages within the villages, but was unable to locate an address in the smaller village for his final parcel. The house had a name, but no number. It had to be close. Granville looked round hoping to see, maybe a young lady with a pram, or an old man on a bicycle, who could help him. Country people know who lives where within their villages. And although there was nobody pushing a pram or riding a bicycle, as he rounded a corner in a narrow lane, there were two riders on horseback. One pulled onto the bank beside the road, which provided space to pass, as well as an obvious opportunity.

"OI! 'Scuse me," Granville bellowed through his open window. "D'you know where Rose Cottage is please?"

It was a cold, frosty morning, and the rider had a scarf around the lower part of her face. As she pulled the scarf down in order to reply, Granville's jaw dropped a foot or two, and the other rider looked daggers at him.

"Continue to the end of this lane, turn right, and it's the third cottage on the left behind a high hedge," said Her Majesty.

"Thank you, Ma'am," gasped Granville, and moved off smartly down the lane. One wonders if maybe the Queen turned to her security officer and said, "Normal for Norfolk, my dear. Normal for Norfolk."

Back at the depôt, Granville could hardly contain himself. He told one or two workmates, and word spread through the workforce. His manager telephoned the *Eastern Daily Press*, and the story soon appeared in print, and also in the national news magazine produced by the company.

More recently a friend of mine brought a plumber to one of our businessmen's dinners. "His name is Gren. It's short for Grenville, but everyone calls him Gren," said Frank. And then a really strange coincidence, when Gren said, "My brother-in-law is called Grenville too. I married his sister, you see. And he's famous in the family, and in a way, in Norfolk, cos he kinda met the Queen when he was in Dersingham one day." He paused and grinned broadly, and added, "Well, kinda."

As a footnote, the Royal Family are particularly fond of their 20,000 acre country retreat at Sandringham, and traditionally spend Christmas there. In fact, the Queen usually spends around two months in residence at that time of year, including the anniversary of her father's death in early February. Both her father, George Vl, and her grandfather, George V, died there. It was the setting for the first Christmas broadcast, by George V in 1932. In 1977, for the Silver Jubilee, the Queen opened Sandringham House to the public for the first time.

Unlike Buckingham Palace and Windsor Castle, Sandringham House (and Balmoral) are the Queen's private residences.

Although my city practice was around fifty miles from Sandringham, the Queen's chaplain became a patient, and invited my family to visit for a conducted tour of the chapel. At that time, I had three small daughters. "This is where Prince Charles sat, just two weeks ago," the young chaplain said. "You can hold his prayer book - the one that he was holding, if you like. Here, take it." A memorable moment for the girls. And for my wife and me.

The small village of Anmer, where Granville delivered a package and met the Queen, is situated just two miles from Sandringham House. Anmer Hall, a beautiful Georgian country house situated on the Sandringham estate, was given to the Duke and Duchess of Cambridge by the Queen, as a wedding present.

****

My father's cousin Derrick worked in the family business in Peterborough. They were tailors. When his father passed on, Derrick realised the value of the business, and he was soon described by his friends as 'young retired'. Those were the days when Volkswagen Dormobiles started appearing on our roads, and one was driven by cousin Derrick. His adventures became legendary within the family, as he explored the length and breadth of Great Britain, before venturing further afield into Europe. He loved Norfolk, often visited us, and when a plot of land in Walcott-on-sea came on the market, bought it and had plans drawn up for a bungalow. This was duly constructed by Fred Spragg, a local builder with foreman

Charlie and his workforce of two or three local tradesmen. Derrick took the plans and measurements to a carpet retailer, and placed an order for every room. Shortly after the building was completed, the carpet company arrived, but encountered problems. In a number of rooms, the carpets were too big, and the fitters had to remove excess material where appropriate in order to get them to fit properly. However, in the sitting room, the carpet was significantly short. Derrick phoned Fred, who drove straight to the site. He apologised profusely, and explained, "If I've told Charlie once, I've told him a thousand times, 'Measure it, man. Measure it. Don't pace it out. Measure it.' Wait till I see Charlie." So Fred called the carpet company, and everything was put right. Later, my cousin Derrick learnt from his neighbours that this was just 'Normal for Norfolk'.

BL

"Could you call Mrs. Death through to the surgery, please?" I asked my nurse. She hesitated, and then smiled. "I think she will pronounce it 'Deeth'", said Tracey. I might have lived in the county for longer than my nurse, but I had never encountered this name, whereas she had presumably had brushes with Death before. The receptionist at my city practice, Daphne, had always lived in the county, and later informed me that there were quite a number of Deaths in Norfolk. She had heard that the name was a corruption of De'ath, or de'Ath, and of French origin. I have read that it probably originated from Flanders, and it is possible that people of that name arrived here with the Huguenots in the 17th

187

century during their persecution on the continent. "And they insist on being called Deeth," said Daphne, "and not Death." I understand that the name is more widespread, but I have only come across it in Norfolk. "Quite normal in Norfolk,' said Daphne.

Until the Norman conquest, there were no surnames. If a boy was named Tom by his father, he was Tom. If there were other boys called Tom, he might be known as John's Tom, or Harold's Tom, or Peter's Tom. But after the Norman invasion in 1066, surnames started to be used. They often involved the father's name, and so there was Johnson (corruption of John's son), Harrison (Harry's son) and Peterson (Peter's son). And other similar contractions. Or they could be occupational, such as Baker and Taylor. Hill, Vale and Woods would be geographical, while Small, Large, and Grossman were derived from physical attributes. At school, there was a boy called Bumfrey, and we could all see why that family had acquired their surname. Poor lad.

But with literally thousands of patients, I came across a huge variety of surnames, some of which I had not encountered outside the county.

"I see we have the Tortice family in this morning," said Amanda, the nurse at my county practice.
"Sounds like we're playing *Happy Families* to me," I replied.
"There's ever so many Tortices in the town," she said. And that was indeed the case. And I was not the first person to jump to a wrong conclusion concerning the spelling of the surname Tortice.

John Kett was headmaster of a school in Cawston, around seven miles from my county practice. He had moved there from outside Norfolk, and came to me as a patient. He related an incident that he had found embarrassing at the time, though he later came to view it as highly amusing. He was still relatively new at the school, when there was a Parent Teacher Association evening.

"Headmaster, this is Mrs. Tortice. Three of her children are pupils here," said a member of staff. This was a new name to John, and he thought it most unusual. He wondered if it might be spelt t-o-r-t-o-i-s-e but on looking through the school records, realised it was t-o-r-t-i-c-e. Later that week, he was strolling through the main street in the village of Cawston, quite close to where the school was situated, when round the corner ahead of him walked the lady with the unusual name. She smiled at him as she approached, and John suddenly found his mind had gone completely blank. She was barely ten yards away and he was really struggling now. Suddenly his mind seemed to clear, and in response to, "Good afternoon, Mr. Kett" from the parent, the headmaster replied, "And good afternoon to you too, Mrs. Hedgehog." Thirty seconds later he stopped dead in his tracks and froze. *Not* Hedgehog - *Tortice.*

EH

A television series in the 1990s caused the surname Bean to bring a smile to people's faces, and so this is obviously not exclusively a Norfolk surname. However, again in the town where my county practice was situated, there was an abundance of Beans. One could say that the town was full of Beans. In one of the television programmes, Mr. Bean went to the dentist, where he experimented with the equipment whilst the dentist was out of the surgery, and tried to treat his own teeth. I went through to the waiting room to call my next patient, Mr. Bean, through for treatment. He had not turned up, and there was silence, until some wag volunteered, "He's doing his own teeth these days!" Suddenly the room was alive with laughter.

Interestingly, one of the most common surnames in Norfolk in the nineteenth century was Raspberry. But I have yet to come across anyone anywhere called Raspberry. Even in Norfolk, I have not come across a Raspberry.

Finally, in common with every other county in the British Isles, we have our own way of pronouncing the names of some of our towns and villages. And this has nothing to do with the Norfolk accent. So Wymondham is pronounced *Windum,* Mundesley is *Munsly* and Happisburgh is *Hazebrer.* Stiffkey is a north Norfolk coastal village first mentioned in the Domesday Book, and literally means 'stump island'. The Norfolk pronunciation is *Stewkey.* The village is as famous for its cockles, as Cromer (locally pronounced *Croomer*) is for its crabs. And the county itself? - *Norfork.* So real Norfolk people say, *Normal for Norfork.*

PH

Chapter Twelve

Norfolk Churches - and my journey

Jumble sales, Flemish weavers, canaries, Malchus' ear.

As the preacher droned on in a solemn monotone, most eyes closed and chins gently rested on chests. The small elderly congregation in the country chapel in rural Norfolk appeared to have departed for the antediluvian land of Nod - except for Jack, sitting alone in the back row. His flushed face was deepening in hue as he became increasingly agitated, and eventually leaving his pew, he strode to the shelves of Bibles and hymn books at the rear of the building. He quickly found the largest and heaviest tome, and removed it from the shelf. With the athletic prowess of an Olympic shot putter, he took aim at the preacher and hurled the huge volume high in the air. It rotated slowly as it flew over the heads of the oblivious congregation, on its ominous trajectory towards the unsuspecting target, whose eyes remained glued down onto his preaching notes. Alas, with the passing of years there had been an accompanying passing of strength, and the missile fell short of its target, landing with a loud thump on the back of the head of a balding octogenarian dozing in the front row. Knocked off his seat, he crashed to the ground, hearing aids skidding east and false teeth slithering west across the tiled floor. Now at last there was something to grab the attention of the congregation, who creaked to their feet and shuffled round the motionless victim. "Are yer awlroight?" enquired the senior steward. "Can yer hair me? Can yer speak?" The prone figure stirred slightly, and turning his head, stammered out, "Not hard enough. I can still hear him!"

I have always enjoyed a sense of humour, and the story I have just related was one of my favourites. I was sure it was not really true, but it was not too far removed from my regular Sunday morning experience. My parents' childhood years had included church on Sundays. People did so when my parents were young, and no doubt, there were those who really wanted to worship, and there were those who attended under duress. Like me in the late 1950s. My father had been a happy, contented man looking after the garden on Sunday mornings. I had spent my Sundays collecting creatures suited to my bedroom menagerie. My young sister had her dolls. So why spoil it all with church?

My mother was the dominant force in our family, partly due to my father's accident, which I described earlier. She felt an affinity for the Congregational denomination that had been an integral part of her childhood years. And having discovered there was a church of her chosen persuasion in North Walsham, she announced that we would all be attending in future. Two of us protested, my sister kept her head down and played with those dolls, and my mother was, as I have said, the dominant force.

The lady minister's sermons grew lengthier every week. I complained to my mother, who was not interested. I pressed, and proved my point by constructing histograms (a type of graph), but to no avail.

I asked some of the older ladies (most of the congregation were ladies, and elderly. Or old) if they really believed in God. They told me they were 'seeking', and I felt that if they had not 'found' during their eighty or more years on this earth, then they might as well give up. And was there not a Bible verse about asking, seeking and knocking, and did they not feel rather let down?

One Sunday morning, the lady minister came through to the Bible study class, which comprised my sister and me. She said she wanted us to know that God was a God of love, and hell did not really exist. So the Bible was not true? Or maybe just the Ten Commandments and the luvvy bits were? Who decided which parts to believe? More and more, the church confirmed me in my atheism.

And then there was the endless succession of jumble sales. Jumble - and at last members of the congregation came to life. Jumble - so there was something that brought a smile to the faces of our agéd congregation. Jumble - so that's what it was all about.

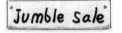

BL

As a young teenager, I cycled miles every week, enjoying adventures of a rural nature that could never be understood by townies. To search for owl pellets under ancient oaks, and the thrill of discovery. (Owls feed largely on small rodents, which they swallow whole. Their digestive system absorbs the meat, and then regurgitates the fur and bones as a pellet. They usually do this perching high on a branch, and regularly choose the same site. How can I possibly describe the sheer delight with which an enthusiast will dissect such pellets, seeking to identify the owl's recent diet from the bones and fur one finds within?). I would pass churches. They had high towers and long naves, with porches and buttresses, and were an unforgettable feature of villages and indeed, of rural landscapes relatively remote from the communities they served. I would cycle past, perhaps with dead coypus swinging from my handlebars, or live mice in my jacket pockets.

Norfolk has outstandingly fine church buildings, which are a legacy from the prosperous days of the Flemish weavers. Until the 18th century, Norwich had been the second city in the land. In the 13th century, wool was exported to the Flemish weavers. Amsterdam was one day's sailing away, whilst the road journey to London took four days. And then in the 16th and early 17th century, Flemish weavers arrived here, escaping the inquisition of the Spanish-ruled Netherlands. They brought with them canaries, the breeding of which became a feature of the city of Norwich. That industry has ceased, but the tradition lives on with Norwich City football team wearing green and yellow strip, and being known universally as the Canaries. They also constructed Dutch barns, which continue to be a feature of the region, as do Dutch gables – both step gables and bell gables are very common. The whole county prospered, and the resulting huge churches are a feature of rural Norfolk.

BL

Typically, the tiny, but picturesque, village of Worstead, which gave its name to the cloth, has a magnificent church out of all proportion to the size of its small community. In fact, over 1,000 medieval churches were built in the county, and 659 still stand, the greatest concentration in the world. Because of their history, they are sometimes referred to as the wool churches.

Historic traditional Norfolk churches. I love them. They are beautiful, awesome, and a part of the character of our Norfolk landscape. We have more round-towered Saxon churches than any other part of England, and our native flint was used in the building of so many.

BL

Norwich cathedral is Norman, and its construction was started in 1096, around thirty years after the castle was founded on the orders of William the Conqueror. Some churches have elevated, commanding positions, and are landmarks, not least when hiking in the county. Others are secluded and hidden within a screen of mature trees, and a serendipity to come across.

Rounding a bend on a tree-lined lane, and unexpectedly finding myself pedalling past a quaint country chapel, I would sometimes recall another story concerning a fabled preacher, once active within the agricultural community of Norfolk.

Fred Dodsworth had been a chapel preacher for years. Indeed decades. Maybe there would be just six in the congregation, and he would need to cycle several miles to join them, but he felt called to preach. And preach he did. However, there was a problem, and Fred himself seemed oblivious to it. Like so many preachers, he had his favourite texts and favourite stories. Fred just loved the story of Peter drawing his sword in the garden of Gethsemane, and cutting off the ear of the high priest's servant, called Malchus. Whether he was preaching on love, or prayer, or heaven, or hell, or almost any subject,

Fred would illustrate with, "Like when Peter drew his sword, and..." or, "This reminds me of how Malchus lost his ear, when..." or, "I remember how Peter once tried to defend Jesus, drawing his sword..."

The preaching was quite good, but the predictable references to the sword and the ear became a talking point. A distraction. A joke. And the time came when the regional leadership was approached concerning this apparent obsession. They met together, and discussed the problem at some length, until an elderly man of great wisdom came up with a foolproof solution. "We'll git 'im to do an 'arvest festivool service," said Herbert Yaxley. "Jist shoo me 'ow 'e can bring the sword and the air into thet?" And so it was agreed, and Fred was invited to preach at the Harvest Festival service at Little Rumpington. Word got round, diaries were marked, and on the day itself, a multitude attended.

Stewards, elders and regional leaders were shoulder to shoulder in the back pew, and every seat in the chapel was taken. As Fred embarked on his Harvest Festival sermon, everyone remained awake, alert in fact, and hanging on every word. Victory! Poor Fred - how could Fred possibly introduce Peter's sword and Malchus' ear into a Harvest Festival service? In fact, perhaps Fred couldn't, and certainly Fred didn't. The sermon ended, and the stewards, elders and regional leaders looked round at one another, nodded, smiled, and sat back, waiting for the final hymn.

"And our final hymn this morning is number five hundred and fourteen. Let us sing together this wonderful Harvest Festival hymn, 'Come, ye thankful people come, Raise the song of harvest home.'" Fred paused. He then fixed his eye on the smug expressions of stewards and others in the back row. There was the hint of a mischievous smile, and a twinkle in his eye, as he added, "And I would particularly draw your attention to the fifth line of the second verse, where we read, 'First the *blade*, and then the *ear*.'" Fred's face broke into a huge grin, and appreciating the wit of the man, the congregation sang robustly, and with Herculean gusto, "First the BLADE, and then the EAR"!

****

I would like to briefly relate my personal spiritual journey, after which I shall take a broader look at Norfolk church buildings together with a few memories.

Although not born into a church-going family, from youngest childhood I was taught the stories of Jesus both at home and at school. And I mindlessly accepted them. I was a child.

As a church-attending adolescent, I entered grammar school where I was taught Darwin's theory of evolution. I mindlessly accepted *that*. Well, the person teaching me was an erudite schoolmaster, and I was a lowly pupil. Creation? God? I could not reconcile such beliefs with my new understanding of evolution. I became an atheist. A church attending atheist, like the choir master, who told us all that he had no belief whatsoever in God, but did enjoy singing.

A few days short of my nineteenth birthday, I climbed aboard the train to London, dragging two heavy suitcases behind me. Ahead of me were five years of studying, injecting, drilling and filling, not to mention extractions, crowns, bridges, and so much more. But I was convinced that I had evolved from monkeys, which themselves had developed over millions of years from chemical blobs in a primeval ocean. Some years later I was told that if you believe your ancestors were monkeys, then you are liable to behave accordingly. And in measure I did, which, in my second year in London, resulted in me receiving twenty-four hours' notice to get out of the University hall of residence that had been my home for fifteen months. Details in a previous book!

I had four really special grandparents and loved them all. My maternal grandfather was a successful businessman, and successful in everything else too. If I ever wanted a rôle model in life, I looked no further than Grandpa. But he did not believe that he was descended from monkeys (as far as I know) and had very little in common with them. I respected him tremendously, and when he asked me to find a church and go there when in London, my heart sank. That was something I was escaping from. But I loved and revered Grandpa, and did find a church of our family's denomination, and trotted along from time to time. Frankly, it was not much more inspiring than the one I had left. But, to their credit, they never mentioned jumble sales.

I was at a freshers' social the first week of my first term at the London Hospital. ('Freshers' are first year students, new to the University). Around a dozen of us stood in a tight circle, each with a pint in our hand, and bragging away as young men do. And then, taking us totally by surprise, a medical student said, "But Jesus Christ has changed my life." There was silence. I thought to myself, 'You're training to be a doctor. Mate, you need to see one. Fast.' And then we were all talking again. But I never forgot that young man's interjection.

It was the '60s. Parties, loud music, Beatles, Stones, Animals. Beer, more beer, and then some more. I spent time training at the hospital, and evenings studying, but - I wanted to live with a capital 'L', and surely parties, alcohol, girls were the way to real fulfilment in life. I was burning the candle at both ends, as we used to say.

BL

Part way through my second year, I felt I was nearing a breakdown. Stress. I went to the students' doctor, who sent me to the students' psychiatrist, and he put me on *Librium*. Like so many others. And shortly after that, I bumped into an old girlfriend from my first year, who told me that Jesus Christ had changed her life. And from that moment, the *God Squad*, as I called them, were everywhere. I could not get away from them, and actually, they were rather nice people. Deluded, and obviously needing faith as a crutch, I thought - but unfortunately, thoroughly decent people. They were not like the jumble sale brigade, nor like those at the church I had attended (sometimes) in central London. So why did they claim that their lives had been changed, that their prayers got answered, and that they knew God?

I have covered my response to these encounters elsewhere, so suffice to say that I quizzed them, confronted them, read parts of the Bible, and even sent up the occasional prayer. Then, one day in October 1965, I sensed the presence of God in my room. This was something totally new. I felt smug. I now knew what many others did not. And then I responded, with a form of surrender, and enlisting. A rather disappointed young man became a very fulfilled individual. Again, I have covered this elsewhere, but it leads on to further later experiences in Norfolk churches.

Warming a pew in a traditional church was never going to be the way for me. My whole life had changed. I had stopped swearing almost instantly, which some of my friends must have found quite sad. And my values changed, which no doubt brought further lamentation. And what the Lord had done for me, he could do for others, and although after 1968 I was a practising dental surgeon, I was also speaking of my new life in churches of all denominations and none. That spiritual journey continues today, and is covered in other books that bear my name.

****

Churches, chapels and cathedrals did not shout out to me for attention during my younger years. But in Norfolk, they cannot be ignored. They are an integral feature of our landscape, and as I have already stated, even a teenager returning from tracking and trapping rodents large and small was not oblivious to the magnificent architectural wonders he was pedalling past.

A number of village churches are quite outstanding, and yet are relatively unknown, even within the county. On several occasions I have cycled past the church of St. Peter and St. Paul in the parish of Salle. Pronounced Saul. The *Norfolk Churches* website is invaluable in giving both description and background to the Anglican churches of the county. Salle Church is described as being seen long before you arrive, and depicted as a great tower rising out of barley fields in the middle of Norfolk, with just a couple of Victorian buildings and a cricket pitch for company. That is a beautiful description, and has been my own experience whilst pedalling along nearby country lanes.

It is huge, and especially so relative to the small community it serves. As a curly-haired lad exploring the Norfolk countryside on two wheels, Snowball took much of the landscape for granted. And yet - why did I encounter such enormous, magnificent buildings so frequently on these expeditions? In fact, as I have already stated, they are medieval and therefore pre-Reformation, and were financed by patrons, partly in anticipation of prayers for their *post mortem* welfare. The wealth created by the Flemish weavers was also significant in the construction of such buildings.

It was in the mid-1950s that my parents would take us on excursions to Norwich, where we would go from shop to shop, trying on shoes, or trousers, or watching my mother and sister do so. Except neither wore trousers. "Ladies don't," said mother. Such shopping trips were so boring, and yet there was respite. The city of Norwich is dominated by two Norman buildings - the castle and the cathedral. The castle dates from shortly after 1066 and stands in a commanding position, overlooking the city. My parents took my sister and me on a tour of the museum housed there, as indeed I have taken both my children and grandchildren.

"Cor Daddy, is that where they hanged Robert Kett? Right up there, at the top?" At school I had been taught about the East Anglian Kett's rebellion in 1549, led by the brothers Robert and William. So this was where Robert actually died. I gazed up in awe and tried to envisage the macabre spectacle. Every visitor to Norwich should visit both castle and cathedral. Back in the 1950s, when we drove into Norwich from our home in

Wroxham, we would pass the front of the cathedral, visible through the 15th century Erpingham Gate; a building largely unchanged in nearly nine hundred years. *Largely* unchanged, though the cathedral's timber spire had been blown down in a hurricane in 1362, damaging much of the eastern end of the building. And there has been damage from lightning and from fire. But always restored. To describe the amazing exterior, interior and surrounds are beyond the remit of this book. Go there.

It was 1956, and I was about to start my first term at the Paston School, in North Walsham. "Music has always been important in our family. If you can join a choir at school, do so," said Nana, my maternal grandmother. I have heard it said that 'unlike poles attract', referring to magnetic poles, and then applying the law in a more universal manner. My maternal grandparents were the living proof. Grandpa did not drink alcohol, nor smoke tobacco in any form, whereas Nana would usually have a glass of Babycham beside her. Babycham? A light sparkling perry, very fashionable in the 1950s and '60s. And in her right hand, she held a long slender cigarette holder which held a long slender cigarette. She would raise it to her lips and puff. Never inhale, but just puff. Fashionable! Nana played the piano, church organ, and violin. I was amazed to hear her play a jig on my eldest daughter's violin at the age of ninety-five.

And so, in September 1956, very soon after arriving at the Paston School, I joined the choir. Which took me into St. Nicholas parish church, used by our school for centuries on Founder's Day and other occasions, such as funerals of previous headmasters. It is huge, with a collapsed tower, and seemed even larger to an eleven-year-old. The school's founder's tomb is at the end of the chancel, the monument having been designed by Sir

William Paston himself. It was our 350th anniversary. In 2006 I returned with my wife for the 400th anniversary, to find my French master, Mr. G. O. Shuffrey (nicknamed Gos, and whose black bag was reputed to contain garlic) in a wheelchair, and now aged 104. I went over and introduced myself - Lawrence B. R. He stared at me and blinked before saying, "So you didn't last long, did you?" Well, only seven years, but it was a long time ago.

Another memory was driving through South Walsham, where there are two medieval churches sharing the same churchyard. "Built by two sisters, who fell out," said my father. "Well, that's what I've heard." Not so far away is Ranworth church, where my children and grandchildren are braver than me, and will climb to the top of the tower, take photographs, and later show me the view I missed. In our own village of Frettenham, the parish church is St. Swithin's. I went to a carol service there my first Christmas in the village, and almost froze to death.

BL

Finally, I'm a Norfolk boy. I was born in the nursing home of All Hallows in Ditchingham. I confess that I found my parents church dreary. Grim. Jumble sales - I never want to go near one again. Forgive me. But having said that, we have so many amazing church buildings across the Norfolk landscape, and my eyes feast on their majestic beauty as Wendy and I so often follow the footpaths and lanes of this rural paradise that we love.

Chapter Thirteen

My Norfolk – Today

Damned foreigners, the Puppet Man, crabbing, families.

"Grandad, you say that you went to the same school as Nelson. Were you actually in the same class?" asked Cameron a few years ago. In fact, quite a few years ago, because he later went to that same school, which had become a sixth form college. And now, following Uni, our grandson is in the police force just south of the Thames. Time passes.

Some things do not change. A brick with *HN* scratched into it. Children playing, the world over. Young men chatting up young ladies. The Norfolk landscape. Since time immemorial, since Nelson was at the Paston School, and since I was there, some things *never* change.

I reflect over nearly eighty years of Norfolk; the accent, the vocabulary, the landscape, Saxon and medieval churches, and the big sky. In these respects, there is little that is different from the days when a curly haired boy, known as Snowball, cycled the lanes and trapped coypus, and was happily ravished, almost, by siren-supreme Carol in the dark tunnel by the North Walsham churchyard. And yet there has been change. Inevitably.

In an earlier chapter, I penned memories of school, and some of my reflections might have seemed almost Dickensian. An infant of perhaps six years old upended and spanked in front of the entire school. Teenaged boys caned so brutally that they screamed, and howled with the pain. Dickensian? No - Norfolk in the 1950s and 1960s. However, taking my own children along to their respective schools in the 1970s and 1980s was a totally different experience. Friendly classrooms and engaging teachers. Colour. Laughter. Warmth. I am generalising, but the change has been dramatic. Caning was abolished in England in state schools from 1986, and in private schools from 1998, following a directive from the *European Court of Human Rights.*

People. There are so many people, driving cars, sailing boats, and jostling one another in the city streets. In fact, just living here. The population of the U.K. has grown so much during my lifetime, and Norfolk has not been exempt. Large housing estates, many of which still remind me of illustrations of *Toy Town*, home of Noddy and Big Ears, contribute to an urban sprawl that has devoured so many of the green fields of my childhood. Yet town centres, and indeed the city centre, are generally unchanged. Norwich library was razed to the ground by fire on 1st August 1994, but like the phoenix, rose from the ashes in the form of the *Forum*, and is largely loved. The open-air market needed revitalising, and the new is, in my opinion, very much in keeping with the design and atmosphere of the old. Those Norman edifices of castle and cathedral continue to dominate the city, largely unchanged for centuries. Meandering through the centre, the market and the lanes never fail to delight and enchant me. Norwich, a fine city. Indeed, it is.

"I've finished weeding your garden, and I'll be off home now," said our friend Dave, one day back in 1975. He had weeded the garden, but also pulled up all of our rhubarb, and thrown it onto the compost heap with the dandelions and thistles. "Come back," shouted my wife, and pointed out his mistake. "I'll put it right," said Dave, and 10 minutes later called out "All done", and quite innocently cycled off home. Unfortunately, he had planted the rhubarb upside down, in a neat row but with their roots in the air. Dave was quite a character then, in his early thirties, and often called round at meal times, and joined us at table. We knew him through church. And now Dave is a star, with an entry and photograph in *Wikipedia*. Locally, Dave is the *Norwich Puppet Man*, a street entertainer who dances with puppets and sings (strangely) to pop songs blasting from his portable stereo player. He is on postcards. He is on television. And he phones me first thing, almost too early, on Christmas morning each year to wish me a great day. Norfolk still has unique characters, and Dave Perry, the *Puppet Man*, is probably the most widely known.

JW

The rivers and broads were busy during the summers of my childhood, and even more so today. So explore our waterways out of season, and enjoy the reed beds, wildlife, marshes and drainage mills, all under that big blue sky. And you'll get a 'roight ole welcome' at our riverside taverns.

The dialect does not change, but in shops and city streets, other accents are apparent. "Too many of them damned foreigners", a market trader told me, referring not to the Eastern Europeans, but to retirees migrating from the Home Counties. Selling their home there, and coming to Norfolk for their closing years, they get a lot more property, and space, for their money.

207

"Go on. See what it will do. Put your foot down *Snowball*," said three school friends, cheering me on the afternoon after I passed my driving test. It was 1962, a joyride in my father's Zephyr Zodiac, and I suspect I broke the speed limit a few times. Between Bacton and Mundesley, we sped past green fields, and in places, a clear view out to sea. That changed a year or two later, and in 1969, the new gas terminal was opened by the Duke of Edinburgh. It processed one third of the gas used by the U.K. and is a huge industrial complex. The use of gas is declining these days, leading to another change in the landscape. And seascape. Wind turbines dominate areas of slightly elevated ground, and forests of them can be seen offshore at many sites along the coast. Hardly an eyesore, but one is vaguely aware of their almost ethereal presence out on the far horizon.

The British seaside holiday became history from the late 1970s, until the coronavirus pandemic of 2020, when suddenly Great Yarmouth was heaving with people again, their West Midlands accents predominating. Otherwise, the beaches are less patronised than during my childhood, with the Mediterranean package holidays offering guaranteed sunshine, nightlife and value for money.

BL

"Hugo. Sebastian. Do be patient. You really *will* catch a crab, I promise you. It's frightfully simple. Just dangle your line in the water and wait." Blakeney quay, Wells-next-the-sea, and Cley have excellent hotels, and are fully booked well in advance.

North Norfolk continues to enchant those who appreciate something more than a sandy beach; fossil hunting, crabbing from quaysides, rock pools, bird sanctuaries, and the royal estate at Sandringham are just a selection.

In 1986 I was married in a Wesleyan chapel. That has since been converted into a private residence. So many have. Others are used commercially. Years later my wife departed for a new life with a new husband on a new continent. Then I met Wendy, who had actually been in the same church as me for around two decades. We married, and though it was the same church, it had a new label of 'independent', and this time the building was a bus station - converted into a church building. And the foregoing illustrates another change in our county, and indeed, nation. Many traditional churches have closed, and the buildings been sold. Young people leave for university, and often do not return. Our society is more secular. Sunday is no longer a 'day of worship and rest', but for many, a day of sport. Many traditional churches have a dwindling, agéd membership, and a vicar, rector or free church minister may well have responsibility for a number of churches and congregations covering an area of many square miles. Some have to close. Many are sold. Meanwhile, a significant number of evangelical churches have increased in number quite rapidly, attracted younger people, outgrown their buildings, and are housed in converted warehouses or purpose-built emporia. Or even a former bus station.

Finally, for so many of us, family life has changed. It was 1963 when I left Norfolk to study dentistry at London University. Few of us went on to further education in those days. I was the first pupil from the Paston School to become a dental surgeon. As far as anyone could remember, or records divulge. Around ten years later, my cousin Andrew became the second. I was told that at that time, approximately 6% of those leaving school went on to University. A disproportionate number of students were from public schools, though that was changing. Now a high proportion of school leavers progress to Uni. Maybe too many. But back in the 1960s, many of those leaving school found work locally. They married within the community. Older people had children and grandchildren living within a few miles of them. Again, a generalisation, but a big change has occurred. Travel is easier and less expensive. Back in the 1970s, one of my patients had a son emigrate to Australia, and would show me photographs of his grandchildren, and try and visit them every five to ten years or so. "Poor man," I told my wife. "What a dreadful thing to happen."

Wendy and I have six daughters and twenty grandchildren. They live in five different countries. One of Wendy's daughters lives in Norfolk, seven miles from us. Her other daughter lives in Scotland. One of my daughters lives in Norfolk, around ten miles from us. The other three live in the Netherlands, France and New Zealand.

"My, you're lucky people. All those foreign holidays, and without paying for hotels!" is something I've heard so many times. Well, the novelty wears off. We love to be with our children and grandchildren, but airports are not a bundle of fun. Fortunately, I am a 'glass half full' man, and enthuse over the restaurants on the ferries both to the Netherlands and to France.

"Hello sir," greets the smiling Philippino restaurant manager aboard the Stena Line ferry, *en route* to the Hook of Holland. "You back with us again? Table by the window? Here's our menu and wine list. So nice to see you again." And on the St. Malo run, staff tend to be French. "Bonjour monsieur. So good to see you back. Zees way plees." And then again, one can ferry the car down to Bilbao, and drive to daughter Rachel in Brittany through Spain, the snow-capped Pyrenees, Andorra, and blue-skied Bordeaux. Great scenery, fabulous hotels, excellent cuisine, and wines to die for.

BL

The flight to New Zealand is best handled with a short break on the way. And so we have toured Singapore, stayed with friends in China, stopped on a farm in North Vietnam, cycled around paddy fields, visited temples, scootered round Ho Chi Minh City, and laid on a sun drenched beach in the Cook Islands. However, I would rather have all six of our daughters, and all twenty of our grandchildren within ten miles of our home in Norfolk. But times have changed.

And so I bring this eclectic tapestry of memories, anecdotes, facts, fables, legends, and absurd jokes to a conclusion. Most of my life has been lived in Norfolk, and the life of the county flows through my veins. If you, like me, are a Norfolk person, pause, linger, observe and reflect. Norfolk is to be relished. Enjoyed. And should you be a visitor to this fine county, take your time. Explore the region. Saunter around our fine city. Put a coin or three in the puppet man's box. Catch crabs. Cruise the rivers and broads. And come back and see us again.

BL

Thank You

Having been born in Norfolk over seventy-seven years ago, and having lived the majority of those years in the county, countless people from this region have had input into my life. And many of them have strolled across the pages of this book.

So thank you to Roger the Rough, Shadley, Grum, Sandra, Ann, Carol, the Hag, cheerful Charlie, fellow pupils at the Paston School such as Gully, Spike, Bog Rat, and schoolmasters Granny, Doker, Gos, and headmaster Ken, who have each played their part. Mrs. Lamb and her boots, June and June, and William, who had a shiver in his finger, have contributed to the texture and rich colourful tapestry of my many years in Norfolk. Not forgetting dwile flonkers. If you are part of that bootiful company of people mentioned here, or one of those I have overlooked, who perhaps talked squit at times, got wrong, and happily engaged with me in a mardle, thank you so much for enriching my life. Thank you to the county of my birth, for helping me to do different, which at times has been absolutely normal for Norfolk.

Thank you, family. My parents (Dick and Brenda to their friends) and sister Julia were a big influence, of course, and are loved and appreciated more than they have probably realised. Being family, being loved, and having rôle models provided a great foundation for later life. My father was renowned for his sense of humour, and not least for his one-liners; it is more than possible I might have inherited some of that part of his DNA. I hope so.

Grandparents provided a warm backdrop to everything family, and I feel privileged to have been surrounded by so many very special people.

Where would I be without family? Wendy and I have six daughters, and each is so amazing. Sarah, Rachel, Naomi and Debs I have known all their lives, and they have consistently been an absolute delight. They have always been there for me, as I trust I have been for them. We always will be. They have encouraged me in my writing, with "Dad, it's like you are speaking to us when we read your books." Wendy's daughters, Fiona and Heather, came into my life with Wendy, around twenty years ago, and so we have less shared history. Though I had got to know their teeth over earlier years, professionally! Our two families have gelled so wonderfully, that grandchildren refer to one another as cousins, even where there is no blood relationship. That is largely due to the loving, inclusive nature of each one of our daughters, to whom we say an enormous 'Thank you'.

Jonny Dangour, *bon viveur,* poet and valued friend read through my first draft, and inspired me with enthusiastic encouragement. He also pointed out a few missing full stops and umlauts!

Barry Harvey was one of the big boys (second form) at the Paston School when I was one of the little boys (first form). I did not really know him then, but our paths crossed again many years later, through a Christian businessmen's fellowship. We are good friends, and after Wendy and I have checked the manuscripts at home, Barry takes over. Maestro of proofreaders, this man goes on to identify and list several pages of unnoticed and unwanted errors of grammar, spelling - and of pure fact. I am immensely grateful to Barry for proofreading this, and all my books.

Derek Blois has been a friend for nearly thirty years now, and has been there with encouragement and support at critical times in my life. He has contributed artistically to previous books, and no less so this edition. Derek has again excelled with the cover design. He has become recognized as one of Norfolk's foremost artist's in recent years, and at the time of writing, is President of the Institute of East Anglia Artists. His work can be viewed at the *PictureCraft Gallery & Exhibition Centre*, in Holt, Norfolk, and online at *www.derekblois.co.uk*

Pauline Hurrell, who uses a dwile, is part of the small church which meets in our home. She also enjoys sketching and painting, and attended art classes given by Derek Blois (previous paragraph). Jonathan Wilson is the son of Angie Myers, who is also an integral part of the church. I am indebted to Pauline and Jonathan for volunteering to produce sketches to amuse, and lighten up the text. I am equally indebted to my daughter Rachel, and grandsons Elisha, Jonathan and Benjamin, who also contributed with sketches. Thank you for these great little thumbnails!

I love our village of Frettenham, which is rich in kind, friendly people. Two of the more senior members of the community regularly stop for a mardle. A car draws up, and the engine is turned off - Roger Goodson gives the broadest of smiles, and passes the time of day. Other vehicles squeeze past, as Roger enthuses over the history of this area - of Dutch barns, Dutch gables, the St. Faith's Fairstead, and so much more. And when Philip Norton stops for a Norfolk natter, no-one squeezes by. The tractor engine goes silent, and with the vehicle occupying 'hedge to hedge' space, Philip grins down at me. His family have farmed in the village for generations, and there is little he does not know about Norfolk country life. I am grateful to these two patriarchs of our community for their knowledge and experience of Norfolk, and influence on my writing here.

You may think that you know what www stands for? Well, in this part of Norfolk, the abbreviation is translated Wonder Woman Wendy. Which is an understatement, coined by some of the hundreds of people who pass through our home, enjoying lunches, dinners, suppers, parties, and general warm hospitality. We have hosted a church in our sitting room for the last ten years, as well as meetings of our businessmen's fellowship, and huge numbers of family. Trucks deliver cratefuls of fayre, and the happy sounds of liquidisers, blenders, dishwasher and fan oven are accompanied by the most bootiful of aromas. For twenty years Wendy has made our home into an amalgam of, at various times, spiritual oasis, restaurant, refuge, sanatorium, party venue and madhouse. I love it. Our home is also a base from which we set out on hikes, drives and various adventures. Yet again, *Crossways*, our cottage-cum-castle, is our retreat from the world, our refuge from the demands of the busyness of life, and a place where we can curl up beside a log fire and relax. In this situation, Wendy is so tolerant as I tap away at my iPad or laptop, sketching out memories and tales of Norfolk past. Wendy – I love you so much.

To you, the reader, thank you for coming thus far. If you have enjoyed it, please tell your friends. And if you have not - hush! But I truly hope that you have.

Also by Barrie Lawrence – Light anecdotal

CURIOUS PEOPLE, HUMOROUS HAPPENINGS, CROWNS OF GLORY

A DENTIST'S STORY

stories by Barrie Lawrence

Published by Grosvenor House Publishing (2014)

After-dinner speaker Barrie Lawrence has been making people laugh - *really* laugh - for years. Now it's your turn to hear his unbelievably funny, sometimes poignant stories from dental school, surgery and life. How did a pet frog lead to a successful career of seven dental surgeries and a bookshop? And of course, he was a student during those years known as the 'Swinging Sixties!'

"A refreshing delight. The author succeeds in maintaining interest by careful selection of anecdotes combined with a light-hearted tone and appropriate pace. I would recommend this book to anybody... looking for something uncomplicated and entertaining".

British Dental Journal, *Review by T. Doshi, December 2014*

PATIENTS FROM HEAVEN – and Other Places!

By Barrie Lawrence

Published by Grosvenor House (2015)

Baron Goldfinger seemed to have stepped straight off the James Bond movie set, Tad the Pole caused the nurses to swoon, while Misty, the flirtatious American lady, suddenly vanished – probably murdered, said the police. These and dozens of other colourful characters walk across the pages of *Patients From Heaven – and Other Places!* During nearly forty years of practice in dental surgery, a wealth of fascinating personalities passed through his surgery. Some were from heaven - and some were from other places! Laugh, smile, gasp, cry, and simply be inspired as you read through these engaging from real life.

"Barrie introduces us to some of the most memorable people he met in this lovely and engaging memoir, the follow-up of his well-received A Dentist's Story. This is a lively read – he has a real way with a tale that keeps you turning the pages. Barrie is a practising Christian, but he doesn't hit you over the head with it; only mentioning it 'as and when' to put his story into context. An enjoyable – and rather uplifting – read".

Eastern Daily Press, *Review by Trevor Heaton, June 2015*

LICENSED TO DRILL – Dentist on the Loose!

By Barrie Lawrence

Published by Grosvenor House (2015)

Licensed to drill! Shots, Killing, Out Cold, Asphyxiated, Agents, Accomplices, Cocaine, the Opposition, The Man with the Golden Tooth, Heroes, Villains and a trip to Russia in the days of the old Soviet Union all figure in this fascinating catalogue of stories from nearly 40 years of being LICENSED TO DRILL!

See just what really goes on at times behind the doors of a dental practice. Three patients fled, one with the dentist in hot pursuit. Fruit pastilles were laced with anaesthetic, and on one occasion, a 'dangerous mongoose' escaped from its cage in the car park. And so much more.

Barrie takes the lid off life in a dental practice in a way that is engaging, entertaining, and totally unforgettable.

Former Norfolk dentist Dr. Lawrence delves into 40 years of stories to come up with his third collection of anecdotes. When it comes to the dentist's chair, all human life is there, and Barrie has met many, many kinds of people over the years; the man who insisted on having a gold filling as an investment (it wasn't) to one who was convinced – like that famous Tommy Cooper gag come to life – that his 'teeth itched' (they didn't). As with all of Barrie's books, this is lively, chatty stuff and a very easy (and rather informative) read.

Eastern Daily Press. *Review by Trevor Heaton, May 2017*

Also by Barrie Lawrence – Christian

THERE MUST BE MORE TO LIFE THAN THIS!
How to know the God of the Bible in Everyday Life

by Barrie Lawrence

Published by New Wine Press (2012)

Barrie writes in his own distinctive style of incidents in his life that can only be described as amazing coincidences – or acts of God!

*A brilliant book by Barrie Lawrence. For anyone asking, '**Is there more to life than this?**' the author reveals a resounding 'Yes'. He shares his own journey of faith with refreshing candour – and then shows how the reader can experience Life with a capital L.*

Michael Wiltshire, *author and journalist, and a director of FGB, the world's largest fellowship for Christian businessmen.*

THE CURIOUS CASE OF THE CONSTIPATED CAT
– and Other True Stories of Answered Prayer

by Barrie Lawrence

Published by Grosvenor House (2016)

A terminally constipated pussy cat, two frozen shoulders, a man with a broken arm, a boy with a deformed arm, broken relationships, work overload, lost at night in a foreign city, irritable bowel, Crohn's Disease, financial challenges, wanting a husband, wanting a wife, not wanting divorce... All these needs were met after prayer. Coincidences? Psychosomatic? Don't be so silly. Come on - get real! Barrie and Wendy Lawrence, two very ordinary people, say, "If He can do it for us, then He can do it for you".

"It's not the most conventional title for a Christian book. But then Barrie Lawrence is no average author. The Curious Case of the Constipated Cat and Other True Stories of Answered Prayer is the fourth book penned by Mr. Lawrence, a dentist, author and speaker. The book is different because not many 'religious books' are written in (his) style. Well, look at the title for a start! It is a collection of true stories of answered prayer, ranging from a cat being cured of constipation, and fog suddenly lifting so a flight could take off, to a troubled marriage being saved".

Eastern Daily Press. *Review by Ian Clarke, 26th March 2016*

PENNIES FROM HEAVEN
How To Get Them and What To Do With Them

Money, Dosh, Dough. We all need it, but – how do we get it? This book tells you HOW! And having got it, what do we do with it?

Is it difficult to make ends meet? Are you on the edge of a financial abyss? Perhaps you really need a financial miracle. Barrie has been in all those places and more, and with Jesus as his supply, has come through.

The Bible has a lot to say about money, and Barrie has also learnt much from failure and success. Using Biblical principles and a wealth of personal illustrations, he shows you HOW you too, whilst avoiding the prosperity cult, can enjoy Biblical prosperity.

Readers will need to be prepared for Barrie's challenges with heartbreak, wealth, financial devastation, time, relationships and "I would never have dreamed of the wonderful surprises that lay in store for me."

Review from Network Norwich by Kevin Gotts.

****